The Minnesota Multiphasic Personality Inventory-2 and Minnesota Multiphasic Personality Inventory-2-Restructured Form: An Essential Primer for Non-Psychologist Mental Health Professionals

Gerald A. Juhnke, Ed.D.

Richard S. Balkin, Ph.D.

DEDICATION

To Deborah, Bryce, and Brenna who light my world, make life exhilarating and rewarding, and bring purpose to my existence—YOU are my life; dad for your never-ceasing love and support—what a blessing you are; Dr. Joseph Oldz THE most knowledgeable and passionate MMPI/MCMI professor I have known—serving as your doctoral assistant for three years and correcting mountainous MMPI profile stacks while learning in your courses proved priceless to my training; "Deacon Erik", "Commodore Will", "Georgetown T", and "John Jay" Allison for your enthusiasm for life and fun; and Shelly, Kris, Cherie, and Donna for ALL your care and kindness.

And

To Melissa, Abby, Gabi, and Izzy

CONTENTS

Chapter 1:
Introduction

Search no more. You've found a book specifically authored for nonpsychologists working in the helping professions Thus, if you are a bachelors or master's degreed child protective services worker, chemical dependency counselor, marriage and family therapist, clinical mental health counselor, social worker, caseworker, adoption services investigator, advocate, recreation therapist, inpatient aid or "psych tech," nurse, or legal attorney or magistrate without specific graduate coursework in the Minnesota Multiphasic Personality Inventory-2 (MMPI-2) and Minnesota Multiphasic Personality Inventory-2-Restructured Form (MMPI-2-RF), this essential primer was specifically written for you.

The book will provide a succinct description of both the MMPI-2 and MMPI-2-RF instruments and will hopefully aid in your understanding of how to interpret basic scores and better understand MMPI generated reports in a manner designed to provide the information you want regarding the exact adult population and clients you serve. Stated differently, the intent of this book is to help you become a better consumer of the MMPI-2 and MMPI-2-RF and promote your use of information gleaned from these psychological instruments to help your clients. It is the intent of the authors to provide a book that will augment your education, professional training, and clinical knowledge with information gleaned from the MMPI-2 and MMPI-2-RF without becoming a psychologist or junior psychologist. In other words, we do not wish to change your professional identity. Instead, our intent is to help you more fully embrace and utilize your professional training and identity while also gaining information on how to best utilize these two instruments to help your clients.

Warning. In the same way reading how to make an egg soufflé will not make you a chef, reading this book will not make you a psychologist or an MMPI-2 or MMPI-2-RF expert. It also will not allow you to purchase or score either instrument. The book is merely a primer to augment your previous academic training and clinical skills and to help you better understand the supervision provided by the psychologist who scored and interpreted the MMPI-2 and MMPI-2-RF instruments you are reviewing.

These psychological assessments are personality tests and are categorized or labeled "C" level tests. State licensing boards have scope of practice laws and professional associations such as the American Psychological Association, the Association for Marriage and Family Therapy, and the American Counseling Association have ethical codes, standards, and professional practice positions that require mental health practitioners to limit use of testing instruments only to those instruments they have received appropriate training, supervision, and proficiency. Level "C" testing instruments like the MMPI-2 and MMPI-2-RF require the most rigorous training requirements and expertise. These frequently necessitate: (a) a doctoral degree in psychology or another mental health profession (i.e., counseling, marriage and family therapy, social work, etc.), (b) formal, advanced graduate coursework in the use of the specific instrument, and (c) professional licensure or certification that allows use of these instruments. Given this book is merely an essential primer, additional MMPI-2 and MMPI-2-RF training via formal graduate academic coursework, test publisher and professional workshops, and clinical supervision and training by MMPI-2 and MMPI-2-RF experts is critically important.

Why write this book? The first author graduated in 1986 with a master's degree in marriage and family counseling. Although the program was clinically oriented and exceptional, he had no formal MMPI training. During both his clinical internship and initial work counseling individuals, couples, and families, many of his court mandated child and adult protective services clients either had MMPI profiles or MMPI summary materials included in their client paperwork or charts.

Additionally, many clients seeking treatment after discharge from inpatient hospitalizations or intensive outpatient programming often arrived with their discharge paperwork that frequently included MMPI profile sheets. Finally, during clinical supervision, case depositions, and dissemination of incoming cases MMPI two and three point codes were frequently used by his clinical supervisors and peers to describe clients and assign cases.

For example, when discussing clients presenting with Antisocial Personality Disorder, it was very common for clients to be described as "high four-nines" by clinical supervisors and professional peers. As an entry-level counselor without MMPI training, I was unable to fully comprehend and utilize the bountiful information already provided by my clients' MMPIs.

Concomitantly, my lack of MMPI training hindered at least in some part the clinical supervision I participated. It wasn't until after I enrolled in my first MMPI course as a doctoral student and served as a graduate assistant scoring 16 clinical profiles, per student, per semester, that I began to more fully understand the utility of the MMPI and comprehend how I could have used previously gathered MMPI information with former clients to more comprehensively fathom their needs and more eloquently intervene in their treatment. This is the impetus for the book.

Chapter One will provide two fictitious clinical case vignettes—one describing Mr. Alex Smith and the other describing Ms. Kenesha Battle Williams. These case vignettes are completely untrue and fictitious. Any resemblance to persons with such names is purely coincidental and unintended. Please become familiar with these vignettes. The vignettes will help readers understand how the MMPI-2 and MMPI-2-RF are scored and how their associated profiles present client concerns and symptoms.

We truly trust you enjoy reading this book. Thank you for your professional commitment to increasing your knowledge and understanding of the MMPI-2 and MMPI-2-RF to help improve your client's lives. Our hope is that reading this book is the first step in attaining the knowledge and training you seek and the professional development you desire.

Chapter 1 Questions

1. Describe what MMPI knowledge and skills you wish to gain by reading this book.

2. Describe the client population you currently serve or ultimately wish to serve.

3. How will you use information contained within this book to help your clients?

4. Who currently administers, scores, and authors the narrative portion of the MMPI's you use?

5. What information do you wish was included in your current MMPI reports?

6. How would you utilize that currently missing information?

7. How could you gain that desired client information via a clinical interview(s)?

Chapter 2:
Clinical Case Vignettes

During our nearly 60 years of combined clinical, supervisory, and teaching experiences, we have learned many important and helpful teaching strategies. One strategy frequently cited as advantageous by both doctoral and master's students regarding our teaching of psychological assessment instruments is the use of in-depth clinical case vignettes.

Our students report when they thoroughly understand each vignette's client and the client's corresponding life history, concerns, symptoms, disappointments, struggles, and interpersonal relationships it helps them better comprehend the client's corresponding test scores and the instrument's application and utility. This is how we teach essential instrument features to our adult learners and how we will present information regarding the Minnesota Multiphasic Personality Inventory-2 (MMPI) and Minnesota Multiphasic Personality Inventory-2-Restructured Form (MMPI-2-RF) to you within this book.

Given the robust numbers of clients presenting with Substance Use Disorders and emotional disorders such as Generalized Anxiety Disorder and Major Depression, the authors' have created clinical vignettes reflecting persons fulfilling such disorders within the Diagnostic and Statistical Manual of Mental Disorders-5 (DSM-5) and corresponding MMPI scores. Our first case study highlights a male client fulfilling the DSM-5 diagnostic criteria for Alcohol Use Disorder and Antisocial Personality Disorder.

Please remember, the described client is fictional and based on an aggregate of clients counseled or supervised by the authors. Given the significant number of court-mandated clients counseled by our clinical supervisees, we believe this case is highly representative of clients served by professional counselors. In addition, it provides a case example that demonstrates the rigid and inflexible behaviors associated with a characterological, personality disorders.

Like the T-shirts we have seen at the beach with a cartoon of a ferocious-looking, sharp-toothed shark that reads, "I don't get ulcers, I give 'me," persons with certain personality disorders, such as Antisocial Personality Disorder and Narcissistic Personality Disorder, often do not find their behaviors or symptoms necessarily noxious or debilitating.

Instead, those around them suffer by the characterologically disordered clients' behaviors. Most often, clients fulfilling Antisocial Personality Disorder criteria are mandated into treatment by the courts, professional licensure or certification boards (e.g., nursing, counseling), or employers.

Many times, personality-disordered clients deny an understanding of the reasons for their mandated counseling or claim the supposed behaviors that caused the mandated counseling were erroneous, mistaken, or "only one time, atypical" events simply blown out of proportion by others. However, as one listens to these client's self-reported histories, it often becomes strikingly evident that the same behaviors, thinking, and feelings that resulted in the current mandated counseling have prolonged histories. These experiences are consistent with the next case study.

Case Study: Mr. Alex Smith

The following psychosocial report is a summary of observations, client statements, and responses made by Mr. Alex Smith during a clinical intake interview. This September 29, 2016, interview was conducted between 1 p.m. and 2:51 p.m. at the counseling office of Gerald Juhnke, Ed.D., LPC, located at One Riverwalk Place, San Antonio, Texas. No attempt was made to verify the veracity of Mr. Smith's statements or self-report. Exact quotations are used whenever possible to reflect Mr. Smith's exact responses.

Mr. Alex Smith presents as a 37-year-old, twice-divorced Caucasian male. He was oriented to person, place, and time. He seemed to have somewhat above-average intelligence given the preciseness of his speech, the sophistication of his chosen words, and his engaging manner of interacting.

Mr. Smith was appropriately dressed. He wore clean clothing, including khaki-colored trousers, an overly noticeable starched and pressed, white, button down shirt, Sperry Topsider-type shoes, and no socks. His personal hygiene was appropriate and unremarkable except for the heavy aroma of cologne about him. Mr. Smith presents as approximately 6 feet tall and weighs about 190 pounds. His appearance was trim and muscular without noted obesity.

He reports being "unemployed" but most recently worked as a "heavy-duty equipment and tractor salesman" for a large, national road Equipment Company headquartered in San Antonio, TX.

When asked the reason for entering counseling, Mr. Smith stated, "I really have none" and "My attorney told me to come, because I beat up my girlfriend." When pressed, Mr. Smith indicated the "only" reason he was seeking counseling was to demonstrate to a judge that he had voluntarily entered counseling.

Mr. Smith stated his counseling participation would result in a "reduced sentence." Mr. Smith reported his recent domestic abuse charge and "other trumped up charges" could result in "significant jail time—I don't deserve that."

When asked about the other charges, Mr. Smith noted, he was arrested on January 3 of this year for "grand larceny and possession of stolen property in excess of $100,000." Mr. Smith indicated the arrest was "a big misunder-standing." Mr. Smith stated the situation was "blown out of proportion" by his former employer.

Mr. Smith claimed the larceny and possession of stolen property charges stemmed from a "jealous boss" and Mr. Smith's "earning more on commission sales" than his former supervisor.

Mr. Smith stated his former supervisor fabricated a story that made it appear Mr. Smith was stealing company equipment. Instead, Mr. Smith reported he was "warehousing" commercial road construction equipment—"backhoes, excavators, and the like"—on his property until he could get the equipment back to the company "where it rightfully belonged." Mr. Smith's scheduled trial date is October 30 in Bexar County Superior Court A.

Identified Treatment Goals. Mr. Smith initially denied any clearly identifiable or desired therapeutic treatment goals. Instead, he reported his primary purpose for attending counseling was to comply with his attorney's recommendations.

However, after further discussion, Mr. Smith reported having "minor issues" related to three arrests within the last 6 months. The most recent August 14, 2016 arrest was for domestic violence. Mr. Smith reported he was under the influence of alcohol and his alcohol use "caused" him to "get a little rough".

According to Mr. Smith he "shoved" and later "pulled" his girlfriend by her hair, but he didn't "break her nose like she claimed". According to Mr. Smith, his girlfriend's reported facial lacerations and "bloody" nose resulted from her "falling" while intoxicated. He denies previous acts of physical abuse with his girlfriend or others, "I'm not a batterer." The other two reported arrests were specific to Driving Under the Influence (DUI). These DUI arrests occurred on June 1 and July 4 of this year.

Mr. Smith stated, "Others constantly get me into fights." When asked specifically who the "others" were, Mr. Smith reported, "Mostly my live-in girlfriend, Catherine." The primary behavior reported by Mr. Smith as leading to his domestic violence arrest was his alcohol consumption, "She pressed my buttons, so I started downing six packs of brew until I couldn't hear her anymore." When asked what three words he would use to describe himself after he begins consuming alcohol, he reports "argumentative," "angry," and "aggressive."

Marriages and Significant Other Relationships. Mr. Smith and his reported "live-in girlfriend" of 6 months, Ms. Catherine O'Donnell, reside at North Hunting Hill Apartments, 1115 NW Cherry Street, San Antonio, Texas. Mr. Smith and Catherine met at Knotty's Bar. She was a cocktail server at the bar. According to Mr. Smith, he made numerous flirtatious passes at Catherine the evening they initially met, and she left with him before completing her work shift that night, "She moved in with me that night." When asked "What three words would you use to describe Catherine?" Mr. Smith responded, "Very sexy, blonde, and tall...did I mention very sexy?" Mr. Smith reported he has "no interest" in marrying Catherine, "I've been married twice before. It [marriage] destroys relationships."

Mr. Smith stated his relationship with Catherine was "on its final leg." When asked to further clarify and explain this response, Mr. Smith said he does not anticipate the couple will stay together "much longer." According to Mr. Smith, he is "tired" of paying the bills without "equal financial support from Catherine."

Mr. Smith reported Catherine is an "addict" who uses approximately $300 per week in cocaine and alcohol. Mr. Smith states he "doesn't trust" Catherine. He stated his level of trust "greatly diminished" after Catherine called the police in August 2016 and charged Mr. Smith with domestic violence. Those charges, as well as other charges that same evening, including drunk and disorderly conduct and aggravated assault to a police officer, resulted in Mr. Smith's incarceration in the county jail.

Mr. Smith reported his previous live-in partner was "Andi." Mr. Smith met Andi at an Alcoholics Anonymous (AA) meeting in January of 2016. Mr. Smith moved into Andi's trailer within days of meeting. Mr. Smith resided with Andi and her two children until "April Fool's Day" (2016).

When asked why the relationship ended, Mr. Smith reported, "The sex got old, and I couldn't stand living with all those whining kids." Mr. Smith denied any domestic violence allegations by Andi and stated, "Although I sometimes got rough with Andi, she never would have filed charges." Mr. Smith, however, reported occasions when he physically struck Andi or pulled Andi's hair.

According to Mr. Smith, these behaviors were precipitated by his alcohol consumption. "I only hit her when I was really, really drunk and didn't know what I was doing."

Mr. Smith reported "four or five" live-in relationships prior to meeting Andi, "None of them were that good or noteworthy." He stated those relationships were "meaningless" and occurred so he could have free lodging, sex, and alcohol, "That's what life is about—finding enjoyment in the here-and-now—kinda a Zen thing." Mr. Smith claimed each relationship "lasted less than a couple weeks." When asked whether Mr. Smith remained in contact with his former live-in partners, he responded, "Why would I do that?"

Mr. Smith married Emma Mae Cronkite during his senior year of high school (1992). The couple had three sons, Cody (23 years old [born 1993]), Kyle (21 years old [born 1995]), and Carter (17 years old [born 1999]). Mr. Smith denied any violent behaviors towards Emma, "Never. She accepted me for who I was."

When queried about the reason for the marriage's dissolution, Mr. Smith reported Emma Mae's father (who also was Mr. Smith's employer at the time) "started rumors" insinuating Mr. Smith's infidelity, "It [the alleged infidelity] never happened. I drank a lot, but I never ran around on Emma Mae." Emma Mae and the boys currently reside with Emma Mae's father and mother in Ohio. In lieu of alimony, Mr. Smith agreed to award Emma Mae full custody of the boys in 1999 as part of their divorce settlement.

Mr. Smith married Lisa McKinney in 2000. Mr. Smith stated, "It was my shotgun-rebound marriage." When asked to clarify the stated "shotgun-rebound" term, Mr. Smith indicated Lisa's father "forced" him into the marriage, "because Lisa was pregnant." Further, Mr. Smith reported he was "rebounding" from his divorce with Emma Mae. Mr. Smith and Lisa lived together from February until May 2000.

The couple wed in June of 2000 when Lisa revealed she was pregnant. The couple separated in 2001 because of Mr. Smith's drinking and domestic violence. Lisa divorced Mr. Smith in 2003. "She petitioned the court and has had my paychecks garnished ever since." Mr. Smith stated, "Just a few more years of paying for that kid, and I'll have my full paycheck again."

Family of Origin and Family History. Mr. Smith is the oldest of four siblings (Alex [37], Donny [36], Eddy [35], and Trish [34]). Mr. Smith's biological parents were Alex "Senior" and Martha Smith. Mr. Smith described "Senior" as a "self-centered, son-of-a-bitch" and "no good, alcoholic." Martha was described as a "saint with a drinking problem." When queried, Mr. Smith stated his first memories of his father were when he was "punched for waking him [his father] up." Mr. Smith reported he looked "more like" Senior than Martha, "I've got his big nose, crooked smile, and small ears"—and had more of Senior's personality traits, "I can be stubborn and ornery like him."

Mr. Smith indicated his parents had a "loveless" marriage, and his father was verbally and physically abusive to his mother and the children. His father was reported as physically absent throughout Mr. Smith's youth, "he wasn't home often." Mr. Smith at first expressed anger towards his father because of this absence, but quickly responded, "Actually, it [his father's absence] was probably best."

When queried about this statement, Mr. Smith indicated father often was under the influence of alcohol when home and would "act violently" towards Martha, Mr. Smith's siblings, and Mr. Alex Smith. Therefore, Senior's absence "probably kept us from getting killed."

When asked about his fondest memory of his father, Mr. Smith quickly smiled and stated, "His [Senior's] absence." Mr. Smith's father died in a "drunk-driving accident" in 1990. Mr. Smith denied experiencing any associated grief or loss feelings resulting from his father's death and responded, "Nope. He never was really part of my life." Mr. Smith continued by describing how he and his mother celebrated Senior's death by drinking shots of tequila after Senior's funeral, "It was a night of inebriation and fun, closing the bad memories of a crappy, self-absorbed father and a violent man who never cared for his wife or children."

Mr. Smith stated his earliest memories of his mother revolved around her crying, "she cried all the time." He indicated that his mother "rarely fed us...she was too busy crying or sleeping." Mr. Smith reported his mother frequently fell and often was unable to stand because of her intoxication, "We [Mr. Smith and his siblings] would laugh at her, because she was too drunk to get up."

Mr. Smith enthusiastically described occasions when he would tease his intoxicated mother in hopes of having her chase him. He reported that when his mother was intoxicated and chased him, she would often run into walls or trip. Mr. Smith stated this was a "sport" with him. When pressed to explain "sport", Mr. Smith smiled and said, "It was sport, man—like playing cards or hunting. I did it because it was fun. If she would have been sober she would have laughed her tail off about doing it to someone else."

Mr. Smith indicated embarrassment during his middle and high school years "because" of his mother's alcohol consumption, "Everybody knew she [his mother] was a drunk—she embarrassed the hell out of me." According to Mr. Smith, his mother has "ill-health" and resides with Mr. Smith's sister, Trish, in a trailer outside Lubbock, Texas. Mr. Smith reported he last visited his mother approximately two years ago. According to Mr. Smith, he called his mother on his birthday last year. However, "She was too drunk to have a conversation. It doesn't matter. I just thought maybe she would have remembered my birthday. I guess not."

When queried regarding his siblings, Mr. Smith stated, "We were never close." Mr. Smith indicated he and Donny had a "strained relationship." Mr. Smith stated the two were in "constant competition" with each other during middle and high school. Mr. Smith reported Donny joined the Army after high school and is believed to reside in Georgia near Fort Benning. According to Mr. Smith, the two have not talked "in years."

Eddy, Mr. Smith's 35-year-old brother, is a computer technician and works for a local community college informational technology department. Mr. Smith reported, "He [Eddy] got the brains in the family." Mr. Smith indicated he stopped by Eddy's apartment on Christmas Eve last year, and they talk "a couple times a year" by telephone.

Mr. Smith claimed Trish was "the real mother of the family." Mr. Smith reported his sister "constantly calls," but he actively screens her calls via his voicemail. He further indicated, "Trish has always taken care of mother." Mr. Smith reported he feels "sorry" for Trish for assuming the caretaker role for "everyone in this frigged up family." According to Mr. Smith, Trish is a "nondrinker" who "tries to save men from their drugs. It's too bad she can't save herself."

Previous Counseling and Psychiatric Hospitalizations. Mr. Smith first began counseling with Bexar County Community Mental Health (BCCMH) when he was 7 years old. Counseling was court mandated. Mr. Smith stabbed a classmate with a sharpened pencil and stole the classmate's basketball shoes. Mr. Smith "couldn't remember" how long he counseled with BCCMH but reported, "It was only a couple sessions."

During middle school, Mr. Smith participated in group counseling experiences for children of substance-using parents. Mr. Smith stated, "It was a total waste of time. I never paid the old goat. He was rich anyway and didn't need any more money." Mr. Smith also participated in "substance abuse counseling" with Dr. Garrie Watts.

Mr. Smith entered counseling with Dr. Watts immediately following Mr. Smith's divorces in 1999 and 2003. Mr. Smith signed a confidential release of information requesting Dr. Watt's clinical reports and a summary regarding those counseling sessions be forwarded to this counselor. In both instances, Mr. Smith discontinued treatment within "three to five sessions for money reasons." According to Mr. Smith, Dr. Watt's "put a collection agency on me, but it didn't work."

Mr. Smith reported he "inconsistently" attended AA meetings from 1996 to the present, "I attend for a couple of weeks. Then I stop once I'm doing better…but it is a great place to pick up ladies." Mr. Smith denied any other psychotherapy experiences or inpatient psychiatric hospitalizations.

Substance-Related and Addictive Disorders History. Mr. Smith reported he first remembers consuming alcohol before age 7, "I stole some of my old man's beers from the fridge and drank so many I puked my guts out." He indicated he has been regularly consuming alcohol since, "By middle school, I was drinking a six-pack or two a week."

Mr. Smith currently consumes seven or more beers a night and mixes his beer with whiskey shots "to get my buzz faster." He stated he used to get a faster buzz, but now has to consume more beers and whiskey to experience the same degree of intoxication. Upon awakening he often craves alcohol and frequently begins his day with "a beer or two—it's the breakfast of champions."

Mr. Smith reported his significant alcohol consumption usually precipitates his domestic violence behaviors and his police arrests. Within the last six months, Mr. Smith was arrested twice for Driving Under the Influence, once for aggravated assault to a police officer, and has experienced interpersonal relationship and work problems due to his alcohol misuse and alcohol intoxication.

Mr. Smith denied the use of other substance or drugs. When asked about his potential cannabis use, Mr. Smith stated, "I sell it; I don't use it. I'm allergic to that crap. It makes me congested, like I'm having a cold or something!" He further denies medical misuse of opioids or other prescribed medications, "Never! Tried it once and had the worst constipation ever. It was horrible."

Mr. Smith denied other potential process addictions such as gambling, "Why? I don't win" or pornography, "I was into porn as a kid, but gave it up. Having sex beats watching it. However, I've probably got to find a new woman to give me sex, because the old one is too focused on getting me arrested."

Educational Experiences. Mr. Smith reported he was "mostly a 'B' or 'C' student" during his elementary, middle, and high school years. He indicated difficulties with authority figures, especially male teachers who challenged him to do better in classes or scolded him for being intoxicated.

When queried, Mr. Smith reported the thing he liked best about high school was "playing football." Mr. Smith discontinued playing football because of his alcohol consumption, difficulties following team policies and rules, and arguments with coaches and players. Mr. Smith graduated from John Greely Williams High School in San Antonio, Texas, with a "college prep type high school diploma." He initially wanted to attend The University of Texas in Austin, but never enrolled. Instead, he attended a local community college and discontinued after a year of studies, "I started making more money as a used car salesman than I would with my degree anyway."

Work–Career History. Mr. Smith began working in fourth grade. He worked as a bus boy at a local restaurant, "I worked 4 to 8 [p.m.] every night." He indicated this work was "a necessity," because there "rarely" was food in his home. By seventh grade, he sold magazines and books door-to-door after school and bused tables at night. In high school, an "AA guy" named "Ed" befriended his father. Ed was a neighbor who brought food to Mr. Smith's mother and unsuccessfully encouraged Mr. Smith's dad to attend AA. Ed repaired tractor engines and farm equipment while Mr. Smith watched, "He [Ed] could do everything and anything with engines." Ed talked his employer into hiring Mr. Smith as a "go-for boy." According to Mr. Smith, this meant he would "fetch" whatever tools or parts Ed needed from the repair truck or garage. Over time, Ed taught Mr. Smith how to repair "anything related to motors."

By the time Mr. Smith entered 11th grade, he was earning $700 per week at the farm equipment company (Terry's Tractors and Farm Equipment) doing the same engine repair work as Ed. According to Mr. Smith, this angered the other older engine mechanics and "Ed eventually became jealous of me, too." Mr. Smith reported the anger and jealousy of his coworkers resulted in Mr. Smith being "framed and fired" for stealing shop parts and tools.

After termination from the farm equipment company, Mr. Smith worked as an auto mechanic at his girlfriend's father's family-owned and-operated car dealership "Cronkite Cars." He worked there his high school senior year. Mr. Smith's speech rate noticeably increased, and he grinned as he described selling his first car at the dealership.

According to Mr. Smith, a customer initially brought a car into the dealership for repairs. Mr. Smith informed the customer that the necessary repairs would cost more than purchasing a new car, "So, I walked him [the customer] onto the sales floor and acted like a salesman." Mr. Smith sold the customer a new car "at sticker price." Mr. Smith stated he "triple whammed the guy."

When asked what this statement meant, Mr. Smith reported he sold the customer a car at the "full sticker price" noted on the car window, sold the customer a "bogus full warranty package" that added over $2,700 to the basic sticker price, and got the customer's old car and title for free—basically, it [the old car] only needed new spark plugs and wires."

The dealership owner was so impressed he immediately moved Mr. Smith from the repair shop to the sales floor. Mr. Smith reported being the "third highest grossing salesperson" during his senior year in high school. When he enrolled in community college, he was the highest producing salesperson at the dealership and the fourth highest producing salesperson in the district.

Mr. Smith worked "on-and-off" at Cronkite Cars from 1991 to 1998, "actually I was selling more dope than selling cars and the dope paid better." He was terminated by the dealership owner, who was also his father-in-law, amid accusations of drinking on the job, stealing, and having sex with customers and the dealership's receptionist.

From 1999 to 2006, Mr. Smith had a checkered history of working as a used car salesperson at multiple dealerships, "plus, I was selling dope on-and-off for friends." In March of 2015, Mr. Smith became a "tractor and heavy equipment leasing agent" at Worldwide Tractor and Road Equipment. In early October 2015 he was terminated from that position amid allegations of theft. Criminal charges of "grand larceny and possession of stolen property in excess of $100,000" were levied against Mr. Smith by Worldwide Tractor and Road Equipment in January 2016.

Legal History. Mr. Smith reported a checkered legal history. He reported stealing "candy, chips, and cigarettes" from neighborhood convenience and drugstores before age 7. He stated that during the times he got caught for stealing, the store owners or police would feel sorry for him once they realized his mother was an alcoholic and his father was abusive, "I could have won an Academy Award for the shows I used to put on for the cops."

At age 7, he stabbed a classmate with a pencil. He later stole the same classmate's "Air Jordan" basketball shoes. Mr. Smith noted that when Bexar County Juvenile Court investigated these charges against him and completed a family evaluation, his mother's alcoholism, father's absence, and the neglect of the children became apparent. Thus, Bexar County Child Protective Services placed his siblings in foster care homes and his mother was court mandated to complete a 21-day, inpatient, and substance abuse program. Mr. Smith was expelled from school for the stabbing and served 47 days in juvenile detention.

He reported, "[After being at the detention center] I vowed never to get caught again."

Mr. Smith reported that the "only times" he has been "caught for breaking the law" since his juvenile detention incarceration were his (a) January 2016, grand larceny and possession of stolen property in excess of $100,000 arrest; (b) June 1 and July 2016, driving under the influence (DUI) arrests; and (c) August 14, 2016, domestic violence arrest that included additional charges of drunk and disorderly conduct and aggravated assault to a police officer. This combination of charges during his August 14, 2016, arrest resulted in his incarceration in the Bexar County Justice Center.

When queried about other arrests or incarcerations, Mr. Smith smiled and stated, "You can check my record. Those are the only charges against me." When queried why the arrests all occurred in 2016, Mr. Smith claimed, "It was a bad year."

Medical History. Mr. Smith denied any significant past or present medical issues. He reported his mother mentioned nothing remarkable regarding Mr. Smith's birth, "not that a drunk could remember anything anyway." He denied any head traumas or surgeries. Mr. Smith reported that his last medical evaluation occurred on or about March 2016 as part of a pre-hire screening physical required by his current employer. He had "no high cholesterol problems on anything."

DSM-5 Diagnosis
Alex's DSM-5 (ICD-10) Diagnoses:

DSM-5	ICD-10-CM	Diagnose(s)	Contextual Factors
301.70	(F60.2)	Antisocial Personality Disorder	Principal Diagnosis; Pervasive pattern of disregard and violation of the rights of others occurring since age 15, including domestic violence, deceitfulness, lack of remorse, recklessness. Pharmacological Domain – Withdrawal and tolerance; Social Impairment Domain – Recurrent alcohol use resulting in a failure to fulfill major role obligations at work and home; Continued alcohol use despite recurrent interpersonal problems; Impaired Control Domain – History of unsuccessful efforts to cut down or control alcohol use; Significant time spent obtaining, using, and recovering from alcohol effects.
303.90	(F10.20)	Alcohol Use Disorder, Severe	
995.81	(T74.11XD)	Spousal Violence, Physical Confirmed	Recurrent domestic violence

Alex's intake assessment interview provides a clinical picture of a man fulfilling Antisocial Personality Disorder and struggling with Alcohol Use Disorder. Personality and alcohol problems have permeated his life. This is especially evident in Alex's marriage and chronic histories of substance use, violence, and police interactions.

Mr. Smith's intake assessment interview provides interesting factors which contribute to his DSM-5 Diagnosis. Mr. Smith's stated reason for entering counseling was, "My attorney told me to begin counseling, because I beat up my girlfriend." Basically, none of Mr. Smith's concerns are pressing for him. His drinking, arrests, and upcoming court trial are not perceived by Mr. Smith as exceptionally problematic. His primary reason for engaging in counseling at this time is compliance to his attorney's directions. Therefore, his DSM-5 reflects his statement and his chief presenting diagnosis is 301.7 (F60.2) Antisocial Personality Disorder.

Other interesting assessment information demonstrates a number of reoccurring themes and behaviors that also warrant discussion. First, Mr. Smith repeatedly has broken the law, harmed others, or ignored the rights and feelings of others; he appears to take great pleasure in describing how he conned or took advantage them. These behaviors began before age 7 and have continued unto today. Multiple examples of Mr. Smith's characterological disorder are evident.

As a youth, Mr. Smith constantly teased his intoxicated mother in an effort to get her to chase him and trip or run into things while in pursuit of Mr. Smith. He called this a "sport" and lacked empathy towards his mother. In addition, Mr. Smith reported stealing candy, chips, and cigarettes from neighborhood stores as a youngster; at age 7, Mr. Smith stabbed a peer with a pencil and stole the peer's shoes.

Mr. Smith later stated he could have been the recipient of an Academy Award for the way he conned police and storekeepers to escape punishment.

Furthermore, it seems Mr. Smith tends to enter relationships with others to obtain what he wants with little attention, empathy, or support for the other persons. Once he has attained his desires, he ends the relationship with little concern for the others or compunction for his behaviors. These behaviors demonstrate an ingrained and pervasive pattern of thinking and behaving that supports an antisocial personality disorder diagnosis.

One of the common behaviors we encounter with persons fulfilling antisocial personality disorder criteria is comorbid Substance Use Disorders. In Mr. Smith's case, alcohol use disorder seems to be commonly associated with his reckless disregard for others' safety. Whether driving under the influence or assaulting a police officer, Mr.

Smith's alcohol use disorder seems connected with his impulsivity and acting-out behaviors.

However, his alcohol use disorder is a symptom of his personality disorder, not necessarily the entire cause of his many antisocial behaviors. Even if Mr. Smith were not drinking, his blatant disregard for others and their safety, his impulsivity and deceitfulness, and his lack of remorse exist.

Unlike our first clinical case vignette, our second vignette reflects someone struggling with General Anxiety Disorder. Anxiety and mood disorders (i.e., Major Depression, etc.) are the most common mental health disorders diagnosed among American adults with more than 6.8 million Americans diagnosed with generalized anxiety disorder in 2005 (Kessler, Chiu, Demler, & Walter, 2005).

Anxiety and mood disorders constitute the largest single portion of our clinical supervisees' caseloads. Many of the clients we have counseled fulfilled the complete diagnostic criteria necessary for such disorders. Thus, given the frequency of anxiety and mood disorders—especially given from the robust increase in clients reporting "anxiety" as their chief presenting complaint since the recent political upheavals and increased attention to terrorism both in the United States (U.S.) and abroad, this second clinical vignette reflects a client presenting with Generalized Anxiety Disorder.

Clients who experience severe anxiety suffer an especially debilitating mental illness that significantly interferes with daily living and greatly compromises life satisfaction. They are wracked with excessive, irrational, and uncontrollable worry. This worry and anxiety permeates their lives. It truncates their relationships with significant others and ruins careers. The experienced anxiety causes such devastation that clients often feel as though they cannot survive. Many contemplate suicide to escape the daily emotional pain and terror. The vast majority of our supervisees' clients and the clients with whom we have counseled have experienced such clinically significant anxiety throughout the majority of their lives.

Ms. Kenesha Battle Williams is such a person. Ms. William's initial assessment intake interview was schedule for 60 minutes. However, due to her extreme anxiety, the intake required nearly 120 minutes. Despite her significant intelligence, she was remarkably nervous and distraught. The anxiety was so extreme it inhibited her ability to adequately focus and fully respond to counselor-asked questions.

During the first 60 minutes, Ms. Williams's rate of speech was greatly increased and her speech volume was decreased and difficult to hear. Her responses to simple, straightforward questions such as "Where did you grow up?" and "What were the most fun experiences you recall as a child?" were rambling, loosely associated to the asked question, and many times rather challenging to follow. Therefore, the clinical intake assessment interview required nearly double the allotted time.

During the latter half of the lengthened intake, Ms. Williams's anxiety greatly diminished, and it became evident via her more focused and detailed responses that she was feeling more comfortable and less nervous.

Below is Ms. Williams's case study. You most likely will want to carefully read her case and be prepared to frequently refer to it as you learn how to utilize the MMPI-2-RF and MMPI-2 in upcoming Chapter Two.

Case Study: Ms. Kenesha Battle Williams

The following psychosocial report is a summary of observations, client statements, and responses made by Ms. Kenesha Battle Williams during an approximate 120 minute, clinical assessment intake interview. The intake interview was conducted by Gerald Juhnke, Ed.D., LPC at his office located at One Riverwalk Place, San Antonio, Texas. No attempt was made to verify the veracity of Ms. Williams's statements or self-report. Exact quotations were used whenever possible to most accurately reflect Ms. Williams' responses. The intake interview occurred September 10, 2017, roughly between 10 a.m. and noon. Ms. Williams was notably anxious during the approximate first 60 minutes of clinical assessment intake interview and continually apologized during that time for her inability to "focus" and "make sense". She further stated, "I hate this anxiety. It just makes my life hellish. I can't even concentrate" and "sometimes this anxiety is so brutally overwhelming that I feel like I'm going to die."

Ms. Kenesha Battle Williams is a 51-year-old, married, African-American female. She was friendly but very anxious with rapid speech, tangential and loosely associated responses to questions, and decreased speech volume. She was oriented to person, place, and time.

Based on the complexity of language she used and the sophistication of her responses to the counselor's questions and the questions she asked within session, she appeared as having above-average intelligence.

Ms. Williams's overall mood was anxious. She demonstrated moderate psychomotor agitation, frequently fidgeting in her chair and changing body positions, and quickly rocking the chair she was seated.

Approximately halfway through the session, she relaxed and she stopped fidgeting and moving in her chair. When she was more relaxed, her question responses became more focused, less tangential, more precise, and far more succinct. However, she continued to demonstrate some psychomotor agitation by frequently wringing her hands and walking around the room while answering questions, "I can't believe I always walk around like this when I'm nervous. I find it annoying."

Ms. Williams was appropriately dressed wearing a clean, lavender-colored, business-type, pants suit, matching white necklace, earrings, bracelet, and ring, and dress shoes.

Ms. Williams' personal hygiene was appropriate and unremarkable. She appeared approximately 5'7" feet tall and about 150 pounds. She looked healthy and appeared somewhat overweight. Ms. Williams works as an "executive assistant" for President Bryson Allen at Bexar County Community College. When asked the reason for entering counseling, Ms. Williams reported "worry and anxiety" and "utter discontentment" with her life.

Identified Treatment Goals. When asked to identify the two most pressing concerns she would like to address in counseling, Ms. Williams responded, "I want to get rid of my constant worry, fear, and anxiety—it is consuming me." Asked to clarify her response, Ms. Williams reported that from her earliest memories she has been excessively fearful and worried, "I have always been too fearful and worried to enjoy life—can you even begin to imagine what that is like?"

She reported her experienced anxiety is not limited to one behavior, a specific circumstance or place, or a single aspect of her life, "Worry and anxiety ruin my life every minute or every hour of every day—I am miserable because of this anxiety and want it to make it stop."

When asked about specific circumstances, events, persons, or places that promote, cause, or increase her anxiety, Ms. Williams stated, "There is nothing I'm not anxious about—work, marriage, life, health, my mother, money." When queried about her statement Ms. Williams responded, "I'm even worried about my worrying. Have you even heard of such a thing? It is absurd. There isn't even one thing I'm not worried about. I hate it." She later stated, "I'm so nervous I find myself picking at my fingernails and skin."

Ms. Williams indicated difficulty performing daily tasks and a lack of concentration throughout the day from her "continuous" worry, fear, and anxiety, "My husband says I should 'stop worrying and enjoy life.' Who is he kidding? He is the major cause of my anxiety and yet he doesn't even know it." Ms. Williams continued, "What I'd really like to do is go on a Caribbean cruise for six months and escape my mother and husband. I can't!" She reported as an only child she "must" take care of her mother, and as a devoted Baptist she reportedly "can't" divorce her husband, "God knows I'd like to leave both of them. It is like being handcuffed to a dead person and a scam artist at the very same time. I hate it."

Asked about the second most pressing thing she would like to address via counseling, Ms. Williams shook her head and said, "Figure out how to earn more money for retirement. It will never happen, because my husband doesn't work and all financial responsibilities fall upon me. This wasn't the way I expected our marriage to work out." When asked to scale her degree of anxiety between "0" or no anxiety and "10" or overwhelming anxiety, Ms. Williams reported "beyond infinity." She then stated, "Anxiety has completely damned my life forever, and nobody cares about what it is doing to me."

Marriages and Significant Other Relationships. Ms. Williams is married to 43-year-old Thomas. The couple has been married 6 years. It is Thomas and Ms. Williams's first marriage. Ms. Williams reports, "Thomas lived with a number of women before me—I think four or five, but I really don't know. It seems he was romantic and caring with all of us at first and after a year or so just doesn't invest in the relationships anymore. I guess he got tired of me."

The couple is childless, "Thomas hates kids and never wanted them. His dad was an abusive, heroin-junkie. He was imprisoned twice for armed robbery." Ms. Williams reported that she thought her anxiety would stop once she and Thomas married, "It [the anxiety] didn't; it only got much worse. I rushed into the marriage thing thinking marriage would eliminate my anxiety. It was a stupid mistake and one I can't change."

After making this statement, Ms. Williams stood up from her chair, walked to the window, and silently gazed outside as she fidgeted with her bracelet and ring. A few moments later, Ms. Williams stated, "He's not the man I thought he was. And, I feel alone and scared because of the intensity of this damn anxiety and a man who will not love or respect me."

When asked what three words she would use to describe Thomas, Ms. Williams quickly said "self-centered", "self-absorbed", and "cold." When asked about her responses, Ms. Williams indicated her husband is physically and emotionally distant, "He doesn't want to touch me or be around me. He doesn't even want to talk with me. Instead of supporting me when I'm anxious, he just walks away and says, 'Get over it, witch.' He is so very cold and aloof. When I am anywhere near him my blood pressure rises, and anxiety and worry skyrocket."

When asked about Ms. Williams's marital satisfaction level, she responded, "Zero. I have no marital satisfaction." When asked what originally attracted her to Thomas, Ms. Williams reported, "We immediately had a sexual connection. Thomas was so handsome, so in control, so gentle. He was the first and only man I ever made love to. I was immediately smitten. However, it didn't last very long. I think I simply got caught up in the love-making and attention." Ms. Williams denies a significant dating history prior to marrying Thomas, "Really, there was no one. I grew up in a Baptist family. My mother did not allow dating. I actually thought dating was sinful. It [dating] was very anxiety provoking for me. I just couldn't go out with men I didn't really know well."

When asked about other significant persons in her life, Ms. Williams reported the most important "living" person in her life is her elderly mother. Ms. Williams reported her mother and her reside together and that her mother is "bed ridden." Ms. Williams reported her mother often is not lucid, "She doesn't even know whom I am when I come home from work, and she grunts loudly throughout the night. It is scary." Ms. Williams hired a Certified Nursing Assistant to take care of mother when Ms. Williams is at work and another to help at night, "It's hard. We used to be best friends. Now, I just watch her laying in her bed, dying. It is a horrible thing to watch."

Family of Origin and Family History. Ms. Williams is an only child. She resides with her husband and mother at an apartment located at 1145 Magnolia Avenue in San Antonio, Texas. Her family, moved from the Rio Grande River Valley in Texas to Detroit, Michigan when Ms. Williams was in elementary school. Ms. Williams indicated her parents were excited about the move, but she experienced "misery worrying about the move before it happened." Once the family actually moved, Ms. Williams indicated she was so anxious she couldn't come out of her bedroom "for weeks...it was horrible." Her family stayed in Detroit while her father worked in various automotive plants.

When Ms. Williams was 14, her father died of a heart attack, "He died at the dinner table." Ms. Williams lived at her mother's home in Detroit until she married Thomas. Once she married Thomas, her mother sold her home and the threesome used the money to move to San Antonio.

At Ms. Williams' suggestion, Ms. Williams, her husband, and her mother decided to live in a one apartment to save money, "If we didn't live together with Momma, Thomas and I could not afford to make ends meet. San Antonio isn't the Rio Grande Valley, but it's nice enough for me. What would make me happy is finding a place to live by myself in San Antonio."

When asked to describe her mother, Ms. Williams reported her mother as a "wonderful Christian woman—the best mother ever." She reported that since mother's stroke, "Mother doesn't talk and is paralyzed...her nurse feeds her through a tube in her stomach. It is awful to watch. I'm basically watching my best friend in the world slowly die." When asked what three words she would use to describe her mother, Ms. Williams replied, "compassionate", "loving", and "kind". When asked what three words she would use to describe her deceased father, Ms. Williams said, "hearty", "loving", and "manly". Ms. Williams described her parent's marriage as "perfect—without one argument or problem."

When asked which parent Ms. Williams is most alike, she stated, "I'm just like my daddy. I have his humor and looks." Reportedly, Ms. Williams' first memory of her mother was "Momma hugging me when I fell off a step at church." Her first memory of her father was "Daddy picking flowers from our yard and giving them to me." She denies any corporal punishment or abuse within her family of origin experience.

Previous Counseling and Psychiatric Hospitalizations. Ms. Williams reported her parents first took her to a church pastor to counsel before her move to Detroit, "I was just so worried and anxious all the time, they had to do something." She denies any relief resulting from the pastoral counseling, "I guess I just didn't pray hard enough for God to take away my anxiety." She reported the only other treatment she has received was from her primary physician who prescribed Xanax starting about one year ago, "I really don't think it is helpful, but I keep taking it because I don't want it [the anxiety] to get worse."

Substance Use and Addictive Disorders History. Denied

Educational Experiences. Ms. Williams reported she was an "A" student throughout high school and college. In high school, Ms. Williams was inducted into the National Honor Society, "that was a big deal for my mother and me. Being inducted into NHS meant I would be able to succeed in college." Ms. Williams reported having many "acquaintances" in high school, but "few friends". When asked to clarify, Ms. Williams reported she was too anxious around others to "be a true friend" and that her only "real friend" had been Thomas. Ms. Williams graduated from First Baptist High School in Detroit, Michigan, and completed her associate's degree in accounting from Wayne Community College. When asked if she had considered entering a 4-year college upon graduating from Wayne Community College, Ms. Williams stated, "No, I just wanted to marry a man, have kids, and be a mother."

Work-Career History. Ms. Williams reported she did not work outside her family's home until after college graduation. She knew someone from her church who owned a small convenience store, "Mr. McGee needed help with his store's accounting. I became the woman in charge and managed the store's operations and finances. It was a great learning experience and boosted my confidence."

Ms. Williams reported that last year, Mr. McGee sold his store and Ms. Williams applied to a posted job opening at Bexar County Community College. She attained the position and is an executive assistant at Bexar County Community College. Ms. Williams reported that to her "amazement" she was hired, "I never thought in a million years that I would get hired and work for such an incredible man". She reportedly "loves" her executive assistant job and "working for President Bryson Allen behind the scenes making everything happen."

Legal History. Denied.

Medical History. Ms. Williams has high blood pressure, "chest pain, headaches, and nausea caused by my constant worrying"; and "sleep problems." She is under medical treatment for each of these concerns and takes the following medications as prescribed by her primary physician, Dr. Kenneth Hiles: Lisinopril 20 mg per day for blood pressure and Xanax 5 mg per day prescribed for anxiety.

Ms. Williams denied previous surgeries, head or spinal injuries, drug use, or medical conditions.
DSM-5 Diagnosis.

Kenesha's DSM-5 (ICD-10) Diagnosis:

DSM-5	ICD-10-CM	Diagnose(s)	Contextual Factors
300.02	(F41.1)	Generalized Anxiety Disorder	Principal Diagnosis; Excessive anxiety and worry; fatigue; difficulty concentrating; muscle tension; sleep disturbance; constantly feeling "on edge"; restlessness; difficulty controlling worrying. Anxiety and worrying are causing significant distress in relationship functioning
V61.10	(Z63.0)	Relationship Distress with Spouse or Intimate Partner	Marital dissatisfaction
V62.89	(Z60.0)	Phase of Life Problem	Client living with husband in mother's home

This case study reflects the types of detailed information gathered during a typical counseling intake or psychosocial assessment. For the purposes of this chapter, it is important to note that the counselor has documented Ms. Williams's age, ethnicity, appearance, behaviors within session, mental status, and home address. Even the client's reported treatment goals are identified.

Furthermore, the typical assessment process investigates the many complex domains of Ms. Williams's life and reflects the synergy between these domains. Specifically, the counselor gathers information regarding marriages and significant other relationships, including Ms. Williams's family of origin and family, as well as her perceptions of mother and father. In addition, Ms. Williams's previous counseling and psychiatric hospitalization, education, work/career, legal, and medical histories are probed.

The intake assessment reveals Ms. Williams's immediate anxiety symptoms are acute, problematic, unpleasant, and debilitating. It becomes strikingly evident that at least some of Ms. Williams's poorer past decisions were made in an attempt to escape her anxiety. Unfortunately, these decisions have resulted in additional life problems and stressors. For example, in an attempt to lessen her anxiety, she married Thomas. Regretfully, the marriage did not bring about her desired outcomes and now even magnifies Ms. Williams's anxiety.

It is important to note that Ms. Williams's overwhelming and expansive anxiety is her chief presenting concern. She likes making everyday decisions for herself without the need for excessive amounts of advice or reassurance from others. She also enjoys making work-related decisions—especially for her boss. Concomitantly, Ms. Williams does not have an unrealistic fear of being left alone when her mother dies. Instead, Ms. Williams wishes she could escape her mother and husband to enjoy personal "alone time." In addition, Ms. Williams likes initiating and completing work specific projects without unrealistic needs for reassurance by others.

Like many clients, Ms. Williams becomes more comfortable as she spends time with the counselor and the intake process becomes more familiar. This lessens her extreme anxiety and allows Ms. Williams to use her precise language. The counselor recognizes Ms. Williams's precise language and understands the correlation between such language and intelligence. Hence, the counselor can make a statement about her intelligence.

DISCUSSION

This chapter has provided two thorough case studies that will be referred to in Chapter 3. These case studies have demonstrated to readers the basic elements contained within typical clinical assessment intake interviews. Mr. Alex Smith presents with Antisocial Personality Disorder and Alcohol Use Disorder as his chief presenting concerns. Ms. Kenesha Battle Williams presents with three identifiable disorders. Generalized anxiety is the most predominant. Thus, generalized anxiety disorder is listed first.

Chapter 2 Questions

1. What additional DSM-5 diagnoses may be relevant given Mr. Alex Smith's clinical presentation?

2. What do you anticipate Mr. Smith's MMPI will suggest?

3. What additional information about Mr. Smith do you want his MMPI results to provide?

4. What additional DSM-5 diagnoses may be relevant given Ms. Battle William's clinical presentation?

5. What do you anticipate Ms. Battle William's MMPI will suggest?

6. What additional information about Ms. Battle Williams do you want her MMPI results to provide?

7. What would you do if your clinical interview and your client's MMPI results were conflicting or contrary to each other?

Chapter 3:
The MMPI-2 and MMPI-2-RF

The MMPI-2 is composed of 567 true–false items and was restandardized by Butcher, Dahlstrom, Graham, Tellegen, and Kaemmer (2001). The MMPI-2 was developed for clients 18 years of age and older with a fifth-grade reading level (Pearson, 2011a). The instrument takes approximately 60 to 90 minutes to complete and can be ordered directly from Pearson at 1-800- 627-7271.

MMPI-2 Reliability and Validity. No psychological instrument known to the authors has perfect reliability and validity, and no instrument is without both supporters and critics. With this said, it is clear that the MMPI-2 revised in 2001 is not without both (Drayton, 2009; Sellbom & Ben-Porath, 2005; Sellbom, Ben-Porath, Lilienfeld, Patrick, & Graham, 2005; Vacha-Haase, Tani, Kogan, Woodall, & Thompson, 2001).

In a perfect world, the personality instrument used by counselors would precisely indicate each client's presenting concerns, symptoms, personality, healthy functioning, and any attempts to distort findings either in a favorable or negative manner.

Combining assessment instruments with thorough and continuous client and significant other(s) clinical interviews, and filtering both with the counselor's clinical judgment and clinical supervision, is the very best way to ensure the most accurate assessment (Juhnke, 2002).

Taking the above into consideration, the authors believe the MMPI-2 provides adequate reliability and validity qualities. In one of the most thorough reliability reviews of the revised MMPI-2 to date, Wise, Streiner, and Walfish (2010) found 1-week test–retest reliability for the MMPI-2 scales surpassed the .70 level on all but one scale for males (scale Paranoia [Pa]) and all but six scales for females (scales Psychopathic Deviate [Pd], Pa, Psychasthenia [Pt], Schizophrenia [Sc], Hypomania [Ma], and RC3 [Antisocial Behavior]). Interestingly, the authors of that review state,

> If the MMPI-2 is taken as the "gold standard," in
> light of longevity, accumulated research base, and
> frequency of use, it is clear that it will need to
> continue to build on the tradition set by the
> newer Content and RC scales
> (Wise et al., 2010, p. 251).

Furthermore, the MMPI-2 appears to have satisfactory construct validity (Sellbom & Ben-Porath, 2005).

MMPI-2 Scales. The revised MMPI-2 has 9 Validity Scales, 5 Superlative Self-Presentation Subscales, 10 Clinical Scales, 9 Restructured Clinical (RC) Scales, 15 content Scales, 27 Content Component Scales, 20 Supplementary Scales, and 31 Clinical Subscales (Harris-Lingoes and Social Introversion Subscales; (Pearson, 2011a). Clearly one needs advanced clinical assessment training to administer the MMPI-2 and all of its available scales. However, for the purposes of this book, the authors will provide a brief overview of the scales and describe Alex's MMPI-2 profile.

Validity and Clinical Scales. The MMPI-2 Validity Scales are akin to the engine that pulls the train. They establish the foundation for the interpretation of clinical and supplemental. These scales provide counselors vital information related to their clients' endorsements. Specifically, the Validity Scales indicate if the client appears to be responding truthfully or randomly to the question stems. The Validity Scales further indicate whether the client's endorsements appear suspect or invalid.

The revised MMPI-2 includes 10 Validity Scales. Specifically, the validity scales are composed of the following scales: (a) Cannot Say Scale (?), (b) Variable Response Inconsistency Scale (VRIN), (c) True

Response Inconsistency Scale (TRIN), (d) Infrequency Scale (F), (e) Back F Scale (Fb), (f) Infrequency-Psychopathology Scale (Fp), (g) Symptom Validity Scale (FBS), (h) Lie Scale (L), (i) Correction Scale (K), and (j) Superlative Self-Presentation Scale (Pearson, 2011a). These scales are evaluated both individually and in unison to determine whether it appears clients were invested and appropriately responded to assessment question stems.

For example, the Cannot Say Scale indicates the number of items that clients did not respond. In other words, this scale indicates both the items that were left blank and indicates whether it appears clients were cooperating in the assessment process. Thus, a client who failed to endorse a significant number of items would end with a suspect or invalid test because of the number of non-endorsed question stems.

Conversely, if a client responded to all items except two, it would be important to determine what these unanswered questions were specific to or regarding. Was there a central theme to the omitted questions? Were the questions specific to depression, anxiety, grandiosity, hallucinations, or violence? If so, it would be important to follow-up with the client to determine what about these questions resulted in the client's failure to endorse a response and what clinical responses might be warranted.

In addition, instead of simply looking at each scale individually, the Validity Scales are also viewed in unison. This provides a more complete picture of the client's investment in the assessment process. Thus, individual Validity Scales like the Cannot Say Scale (?) are reviewed in light of the other Validity Scales such as the Lie Scale (L) and the Correction Scale (K). Here, the Lie Scale indicates the client's ability to present him- or herself in a truthful, balanced manner. Clients endorsing an unusually high number of items on this scale are likely attempting to present themselves in a most positive light and are denying the presence of even minor flaws. Clients endorsing such a high number of positive items may be defensive or may present with a high degree of religiosity or narcissism.

On the other hand, the Correction Scale indicates the degree of symptomatology or lack thereof endorsed by the client. Here, high Correction Scale scores may suggest an absence of symptoms or problems or defensiveness. In other words, these clients are suggesting they have no reason for participating in counseling and life is going exceptionally well. Two ways of using the Correction Scale to potentially identify persons attempting to present themselves in an overly positive manner are to evaluate scale combinations.

For example, when both the Lie and Correction Scales have relatively high scores and the Infrequency Scale (F) has a relatively low score, this suggests the client has endorsed items in a fashion similar to those who are attempting to present themselves in an overly positive manner.

Conversely, clients admitting significant problems will score low on the Correction Scale. These low-scoring clients may be making a cry for help. As in the case with elevated Infrequency Scale scores, clients entering treatment and facing significant interpersonal, legal, and environmental stressors such as jail time, divorce, and job loss may endorse few if any positives in their lives.

Hence, it quickly becomes apparent that counselors reviewing the MMPI-2 Validity Scales can best judge how the client approached the test-taking experience by looking at the both the individual Validity Scales and their configurations in unison.

For example, in the case of Alex, his Validity Scale scores will indicate a higher than expected Correction Scale score and a lower Infrequency Scale score. Thus, when taking the MMPI-2, Alex was attempting to present himself in a most favorable light—a kind, caring, law-abiding citizen vis-à-vis a deceitful, irresponsible, reckless, aggressive, alcohol using, heavy equipment thief who lacks remorse and compunction for how he treats others and who is facing trial for stealing from his employer and being found in possession of stolen property in excess of $100,000.

As you will recall, Alex reported his attorney encouraged him to begin counseling. There is a high probability that Alex's attorney encouraged Alex to enter counseling so the attorney could declare to the Judge that Alex had voluntarily entered into counseling and sought help for his behaviors. Stated differently, there exists a high probability that Alex's legal counsel and Alex have an agenda specific to Alex's entering treatment. The MMPI-2 Validity Scales will likely identify such an agenda.

Clinical Scales. The MMPI-2 contains 10 clinical scales. These include (a) Hypochondriasis, (b) Depression, (c) Hysteria, (d) Psychopathic Deviate, (e) Masculinity-Femininity, (f) Paranoia, (g) Psychasthenia, (h) Schizophrenia, (I) Hypomania, and (j) Social Introversion (Pearson, 2011a). Many times, these scales are referred to by the numbered order in which they are depicted on the clinical profile sheet. Thus, The One Scale is Hypochondriasis, The Two Scale is Depression, The 10 Scale is Social Introversion, and so forth.

The One Scale: Hypochondriasis. This scale denotes bodily aches, pains, and general physical concerns. Clients who score high on this scale are endorsing a significant number of somatic concerns and symptoms and may tend to use these complaints for attention or secondary gains (e.g., being relieved of charges as a result of their physical complaints). Clients endorsing few items on this scale indicate a lack of physical alignments and likely are healthy, younger clients (e.g., 18 years of age) who truly are in the prime of their lives.

Before we move on to the next clinical scales, consider this question, "Whom would you anticipate would have at least a moderately elevated One Scale score, Alex or Kenesha?" Although Alex may have some anxiety about his upcoming court arraignment and possible jail sentence, the authors believe that Kenesha is far more likely to endorse more hypochondriasis items than Alex. Given Kenesha's constant state of anxiousness and heightened anxiety in interactions with others, along with her current life dissatisfaction specific to living with a spouse reported as physically and emotionally absent and living with her mother whom she reports as needing round-the-clock care, one would anticipate that Kenesha would have some elevation on this scale.

The Two Scale: Depression. As the name implies, the Two Scale indicates depressive symptomatology endorsed by the client. Clients spiking this scale with an extremely high score may be making a "cry for help." This could be a naïve or highly dependent client whose spouse left him or someone who may be so overwhelmed that she is suicidal and seeking immediate help to prevent her planned suicide. Thus, the presence of suicidal ideation and intent should be assessed with clients indicating highly depressed feelings on this scale and appropriate interventions should be implemented to insure safety.

Interestingly, someone like Kenesha may well demonstrate a moderate elevation on the Two Scale. Although Kenesha's primary presenting concern is her marked anxiety, she may have a moderately elevated Two Scale, because she feels sad, unhappy, disheartened, depressed, sorrowful, and possibly even despondent about her less than favorably perceived marriage and pending death of her mother. Her marriage has not brought about the support, nurturance, and love that she anticipated.

Kenesha also reports she is an only child living with her mother, because her husband, Thomas, and her could not financially afford living without mother's financial support. Given all of this, one would be surprised if Kenesha did not have at least some elevation on the Two Scale.

The Three Scale: Hysteria. Clients scoring high on this scale tend to demand attention from others, act immaturely and selfishly, and report broad and vague physical complaints. Often, they will initially present as socially able, talkative, and flamboyant. However, as others begin to know them, those who score high on the Three Scale will frequently be perceived as shallow and self-centered, and their once perceived alluring qualities will vaporize as their noxious personality characteristics become more obvious.

The Four Scale: Psychopathic Deviate. This is a critical scale for counselors to understand. Those scoring moderately high to high on the Four Scale endorse items in a fashion similar to persons who tend to act recklessly and illegally, steal, lie, and use other people for personal gain without remorse for their behaviors.

In general, persons scoring moderately high to high on the Four Scale often present as adventure seeking, impulsive, rebels, who have difficulties with those in authority. Typically, they will be substance using, self-centered, and unconcerned with the potential negative effects their behaviors will have on innocent others for dangerous and foolish behaviors such as drinking and driving. This scale is often correlated with antisocial personality disorder.

Given these descriptions and your knowledge of both Kenesha and Alex, whom do you believe would be more likely to have an elevated Four Scale score? Correct! Good Job! Alex is the correct answer. He presents as a full-fledged, high Four Scale endorsing client. This scale also matches his primary permeating personality disorder—antisocial personality disorder. However, be careful to remember that not every antisocial personality disordered person will present as a beer-guzzling, black leather jacket wearing, chopper-riding hellion with a beard, tattoos, and a sawed-off shotgun. Such stereotypical, antisocial personality disordered persons are relatively easy to spot when they are locked in the backseat of a police car after fighting multiple patrons and police officers at the local bar.

Less obvious, however, are those who endorse a significant number of Four Scale items who may present on cursory glance as respectable coaches, prominent business persons, bankers or financial brokers, college or school administrators, physicians, dentists, lawyers, or politicians, but who may repeatedly lie, steal, or place others in social, emotional, or financial jeopardy without concern or compunction.

These are persons like the famed Bernard Madoff. He is a former NASDAQ chair who presented as a highly respectable investment securities company owner. Yet, unbeknown to millions, Madoff operated the largest Ponzi scheme in American history.

These antisocial personality disorder persons are often far less discernable to the general population, until the truth finally makes all aware of the real person behind the mask. Unfortunately, the results of their psychopathology can be just as severe and dangerous as the stereotypical Hell's Angel biker.

The Five Scale: Masculinity-Femininity. This scale relates to stereotypical gender role affiliation. For example, higher scoring males may present with greater aesthetic interests than the general population of males within the United States while lower scoring males may present with a type of John Wayne persona. The later may perceive themselves as robustly masculine and enjoy stereotypical masculine roles, recreation, and interests (e.g., football, NASCAR).

High-scoring females may work in non-stereotypical female work roles (e.g., auto mechanic). They may further present as highly self-confident and competitive. Lower scoring females may fit the stereotypical "Southern Belle" profile of robustly embracing traditionally accepted feminine roles and interests (J. Oldz, personal communications, February 7, 1990).

Most experienced mental health professionals no longer perceive this scale as a true clinical scale. Instead, most perceive this scale as possibly providing further information regarding the client but without the psychopathology suggested in outdated DSM diagnoses.

The Six Scale: Paranoia. This scale is specific to paranoia and trust. Persons scoring high on this scale may present with peculiar thinking. They may be paranoid and distrustful of others. Extremely high scores may suggest someone who presents with active delusions or hallucinations.

However, it seems highly unlikely that a person presenting with robust delusions or vividly active hallucinations would be able to fully complete the MMPI-2's 567 questions. Thus, in extreme scoring cases, the authors would question the veracity of the responses and likely view the results as suspect.

The Seven Scale: Psychasthenia. Clients with moderately high and higher Seven Scale scores typically present as excessively anxious and worried. Many will report they are unable to focus or concentrate and may have physical complaints of fatigue or exhaustion. They are often identified by others as extremely well organized, meticulous, and perfectionist. Frequently, they are highly self-critical and lack self-confidence. Some may attempt to self-medicate using substances like cannabis to reduce their anxiety and worry. In addition, some high scorers may qualify as obsessive compulsive disordered. Based on Kenesha's excessive and unfounded anxiousness and worry, we would anticipate that she would have a moderate to high Seven Scale score.

The Eight Scale: Schizophrenia. Clients with high scores on the Eight Scale may well be endorsing psychotic experiences that could include florid hallucinations.

Similar to the description of robust Scale Six scores, clients with high scores on this scale would likely have difficulty remaining focused on a standardized assessment instrument composed of so many questions. More likely, robustly high scores are indicative of clients making a cry for help. In other words, floridly psychotic clients would be so confused, it is unlikely that they could actually complete the 567 MMPI-2 questions.

Thus, it is far more likely that a client scoring in this fashion is making a deliberate cry for help or seeing to present him- or herself with florid delusions and hallucinations.

The Nine Scale: Mania. This scale describes manic behaviors or episodes. Clients with high scores may qualify for bipolar disorder and may present as grandiose with pressured speech and a history of inpatient hospitalizations.

Nonbipolar-disordered clients with moderate to moderately high scores will typically present as impulsive, flamboyant, socially confident, and gregarious.

Given this scale's descriptors, how would you anticipate Alex and Kenesha would score? Although Alex's score would not be expected to be excessively high, his self-confidence and outgoing demeanor would likely suggest that he would have at least moderate to moderately high scores on this scale.

The opposite is true for Kenesha. Given Kenesha does not present as overly self-confident, flamboyant, outgoing, and gregarious, and given her preferred occupation within accounting, one would anticipate she would endorse fewer items on this scale and have a lower Nine Scale score.

The Ten (Zero) Scale: Social Introversion. This scale measures the degree to which a client interacts with others and feels socially comfortable. Clients scoring high on this scale typically are uncomfortable in social situations and prefer to be alone or with a limited number of very close and trusted friends.

Social interactions are often very difficult for these clients as they are often extremely shy and have difficulty voicing themselves. Concomitantly, they often feel anxious, acquiesce easily, and lack energy. Those scoring low on this scale frequently are perceived as outgoing, extroverted clients who interact freely with others. Often they are perceived as brazen or audacious.

Given Alex and Kenesha's personality characteristics, we would anticipate that Alex and Kenesha's Nine and Ten Scale scores would reflect divergent congruence. In other words, Alex's and Kenesha's Nine and Ten Scales would likely be somewhat opposite of one another.

Thus, Alex's Nine Scale score would be moderate to moderately high and Alex's Ten Scale would be lower. That is because Alex knows how to interact with others socially, feels socially comfortable with others, and is relatively gregarious. This combination of personality characteristics matches what one would expect from a salesperson.

The opposite would be true of Kenesha. Her Nine Scale would likely be lower and her Ten Scale would be higher. This would reflect Kenesha's discomfort around others, her fulfilled generalized anxiety disorder criteria, and her preference for interacting with one or two family members or friends vis-à-vis persons she is unfamiliar.

Code Types. When two or more clinical scales are elevated above typical scores endorsed by the general population sample used to norm the MMPI-2, counselors can use the client's two or three highest scale scores to indicate "two-point" or "three-point" code types. Specifically, these two- and three-point codes provide more information than merely reviewing each scale separately.

For example, should a client's Two Scale (Depression) be elevated above the general response threshold and be the highest score on the client's MMPI-2, and the client's second highest score be elevated above the general response threshold and be on the Four Scale (Psychopathic Deviate), the counselor would indicate the client had a "2-4" code type.

Should the client's third highest score be the Six Scale (Paranoia), and if this third highest score was above the general response threshold, the client would have a three-point code (i.e., "2-4-6" code type). This code would suggest the client would have (a) both depression and anxiety but with more anxiety than depression, (b) resentment, and (c) feelings of dependence and a strong need for affection from others (Nichols, 2001).

Many of the most commonly occurring emotional and personality diagnoses have a corresponding two- or three-point code. However, not all high clinical scale scores result in two- or three-point code types. Most code types, and especially two-point code types, are interchangeable. In other words, the order of the highest and second highest scores has the same implications.

For example, the previously noted 2-4 code type is often indicated as the 2-4/4-2 code type. Thus, no matter if the client's highest scale score was two or four, the general information regarding the client is similar. In addition, should the first and second elevated clinical scales be equal, the results would be used similarly (e.g., 2-4/4-2 code type). Relatively common two- and three-point codes are noted below.

13/31: Often persons endorsing this two-point code report significant physical concerns and ailments. Thus, they often are seen in medical settings. Many times their reported physical concerns are vague and imprecise (e.g., "I don't feel good"). Most will present as immature and demanding.

18/81: Persons with this two-point code often will report delusions and demonstrate thought disorders. They may be substance using and demonstrate explosive or angry outbursts towards others and feel as though others do not understand them.

23/32: Those endorsing high 23/32 disorders often present as dependent and immature. They frequently are unhappy with their lives and find little joy or happiness. These folks typically have hapless life histories. Persons with this two-point scale frequently note work, friendship, and marriage dissatisfaction.

24/42: Persons endorsing this type of two-point code frequently report feelings of depression, relationship problems, and have difficulties following general social rules and mores. Often offenders and substance abusers will have this two-point code.

26/62: These folks are typically hypersensitive to criticism and at least somewhat paranoid. They often perceive others as untrustworthy and unreasonable.

27/72: High 27/72 scale endorsements suggest someone presenting with comorbid feelings of depression and anxiety. Often they are anxious they will be unable to resolve their feelings of depression and are anxious regarding either perceived stressor-specific upcoming events (e.g., divorce, loss of job, etc.) or esoteric future events or concerns of unknown origin. Persons scoring in this manner may fulfill General Anxiety Disorder or Obsessive-Compulsive Personality Disorder.

28/82: Here the test user is endorsing comorbid depression and thought disorder likely with delusions or hallucinations. Common DSM-5 diagnoses with this two-point code include Schizophrenia and Bipolar Disorders.

29/92: Persons endorsing high number of question stems on these scales are likely depressed and agitated. They may fulfill Narcissistic Personality Disorder of Bipolar Disorder.

34/43: Common diagnoses with this two-point code include Histrionic Personality Disorder, Antisocial Personality Disorder, and Paranoid Personality Disorder. They may present as overly dramatic and highly emotional.

48/84: Test users with this two-point code report comorbid antisocial and delusions or hallucinations. They often experience the world as threatening and don't feel accepted. Suicidal ideation is common with persons endorsing this code and the code can be common for sexual offenders.

49/94: Persons endorsing question stems on the 4 and 9 scales match a common profile for offenders and those who are or have been incarcerated. Often these persons are highly adventure seeking, extroverted, and lack feelings of remorse, guilt, or shame for threatening or harmful behaviors. Antisocial Personality Disorder is common among persons scoring this two-point code.

68/86: Test users with this configuration are likely reporting bizarre delusions and hallucinations. They may fulfill the diagnosis of Paranoid Schizophrenia, and typically present as confused.

123: This three-point code is relatively common for persons who fulfill Histrionic Personality Disorder. They are endorsing a high number of physical concerns and may use these reported concerns as a means to escape work, academic, and other responsibilities.

246: Test takers endorsing an inordinately high number of items on these three scales are typically paranoid and may fulfill Paranoid Personality Disorder. They often feel alienated and rejected by others and may well present as argumentative and difficult to interact with.

249: Persons with this three-point code are typically depressed due to being sanctioned or incarcerated. They typically have a chronic history of difficulties with authority figures, the police, and the legal system. They often have social and relationship problems and view themselves as being "the victim" of malicious and hostile others, and they deny or do not comprehend their behaviors that contributed to the noted legal, social, and relationship problems. If the 2 Scale has a t-score at 80 or greater, there is a high risk for domestic violence, murder, and suicide.

678: This three-point code is common to those fulfilling the diagnosis of Paranoid Schizophrenia. Persons endorsing a high number of items on this scale are indicating confusion, delusions and hallucinations, with possible hostile affect. Many times they feel others are controlling them or trying to harm them.

PSY-5 and Supplementary Scales. The MMPI-2 has numerous additional scales that can be purchased and used for specific populations and presenting or suspected concerns. These include the PSY-5 (Aggressiveness, Psychoticism, Disconstraint, Negative Emotionality/Neuroticism, and Introversion/Low Positive Emotionality), Broad Personality Characteristics (Anxiety, Repression, Ego Strength, Dominance, and Social Responsibility), Generalized Emotional Distress (College Maladjustment, Post-Traumatic Stress Disorder—Keane, and Marital Distress), Behavioral Dyscontrol (Hostility, Overcontrolled Hostility, MacAndrew—Revised, Addiction Admission, and Addiction Potential), and Gender Role (Gender Role—Masculine, and Gender Role—Feminine).

The authors have found these scales of significant value—especially when counseling within their specialty areas of addictions, family-couples, suicide, and violence (Juhnke, 2002). For example, when assessing or counseling substance using clients and their families, Juhnke uses the MacAndrew Alcoholism Scale—Revised (MAC-R), the Addiction Potential Scale (APS), and the Addiction Acknowledgment Scale (AAS) MMPI-2 Supplementary Scales. Employing clinical interviews with the clients and their significant others in conjunction with these MMPI-2 Supplementary Scales provides the necessary information to make an extremely thorough and accurate diagnosis (Juhnke, 2002).

Here, for example, Juhnke (2002) uses the MAC-R to provide general information regarding the client's alcohol and other drug use as well as addictive behaviors such as gambling. Given that most MAC-R items are not openly transparent or obvious, most clients do not realize the items are specific to their potential addictions. Thus, Juhnke has found that even guarded, AOD-using clients typically score in a relatively similar manner to those who openly admit their AOD abuse on the MAC-R. Higher scores on the MAC-R Scale are indicative of AOD-using clients and a corresponding Substance Use Disorder diagnosis.

However, it should be noted that clients endorsing a significant number of MAC-R scale items may simply be clients who are similar in personality to AOD-using clients (e.g., extroverted, confident) and may not actually be addicted. In other words, although AOD is exceptionally common among clients with such personalities, such endorsements do not mean that the client is addicted. This is why it is especially important to include client and significant other interviews when making any diagnosis.

As mentioned, Juhnke uses two other MMPI-2 Supplementary Scales along with the MAC-R. These include the APS and the AAS. The APS assesses the presence of personality factors that suggest potential for addiction and addictive behaviors. Like the MAC-R, the APS scale items are not transparent. Juhnke has found that some clients who are not assessed as AOD using on the MAC-R are positively assessed on the APS. The AAS scale items are different. They are highly transparent and query the client regarding specific AOD-related questions. Together, these MMPI-2 Supplementary Scales are helpful in supporting the counselor's clinical judgment and can be used to help establish a valid and useful diagnosis.

Restructured Clinical Scales. The MMPI-2 extended score report provides 10 Restructured Clinical Scales. The first of these scales is Demoralization (RCd-dem) and includes feelings of overall discouragement and general emotional discomfort. Second is Somatic Complaints (RC1-som).

As you will note, RC1 correlates to the original MMPI's Scale One. This scale reports physical complaints and the client's attention to bodily concerns. The former MMPI original Scale Two, Depression, is now the Low Positive Emotions (RC2-lpe) Scale. This scale continues to focus on depression, low energy, and indecisiveness. The RC Scale Cynicism (RC3-cyn) is no longer related to the former MMPI original scale Hysteria. Instead, this restructured clinical scale reports how the client perceives others in general (e.g., untrustworthy, uncaring).

The new RC4 Antisocial Behavior (asb) Scale focuses more purely on the core of antisocial behaviors than the previous Psychopathic Deviate Four Scale. This new scale reflects measures of aggressiveness and one's tendency to deceive and cheat for personal gain. The new Ideas of Persecution (RC6-per) Scale specifically measures persecutory ideation.

The restructured clinical scale Dysfunctional Negative Emotions (RC7-dne) basically reviews negative emotions like anxiety, irritability, and intrusive thoughts. The Aberrant Experiences (RC8-abx) Scale measures hallucinations and delusions.

Finally, the Hypomanic Activation (RC9-hpm) Scale measures hypomania and mania. It reports things like racing thoughts, excitement, and poor impulse control (Pearson, 2011a).

The developer of the RC Scales, Auke Tellegen, by making these new scales, restructured the MMPI-2, greatly enhancing it. His intent was to psychometrically improve the original MMPI Clinical Scales that clinicians were already familiar with (Pearson, 2011a). In essence, Tellegen took the primary central psychopathology of each of the original MMPI Clinical Scales and used the entire MMPI-2 item pool to develop corresponding scales that better matched the underlying psychopathology affiliated with the new scales.

Alex's MMPI-2 Profile

Now that we have discussed the MMPI-2, let's take a look at Alex's MMPI-2 Profile (Table 3.1).

Table 3.1

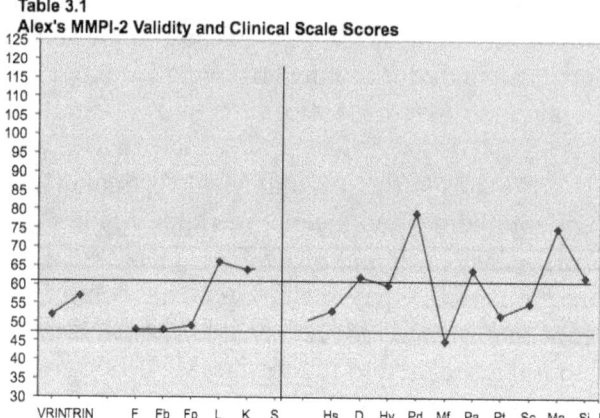

Alex's MMPI-2 Validity and Clinical Scale Scores

We will begin with a brief review of Alex's Validity Scale Profile. The Variable Response Inconsistency Scale [VRIN] and True Response Inconsistency Scale [TRIN] scales measure inconsistency in responses. Given that Alex's VRIN and TRIN endorsements fall between T scores of 50 and 65, it appears that Alex responded to the question stems in a manner consistent with most MMPI-2 test takers. Therefore, it appears Alex's endorsements are interpretable specific to him being consistent in his responses.

Next, when reviewing Alex's endorsements on the F, Fb, and Fp scales, things get a little more interesting. These scales represent "Infrequency" or what used to be termed "Faking Bad." Typical mean scores on the Infrequency scales should be between 50 and 65. Scores 65 and higher suggest someone is endorsing significant psychopathology levels. Scores in excess of 80 are suggesting someone may well be over reporting psychopathology.

Persons scoring very high on these scales may be attempting to endorse severe levels of psychopathology (e.g., depression, anxiety, hallucinations) in an attempt to either be hospitalized or, if a lawsuit is involved, to suggest they have been emotionally traumatized by an event or experience.

This clearly is not the case with Alex. He has responded to the instrument by endorsing fewer psychopathic symptoms than the general population and his scores are just below the typical threshold of 50. Might there be a reason for Alex's under responding?

Before we answer that question, let's continue investigating his other Validity Scale Scores. Next, we look at Alex's L Scale. He has endorsed himself as more virtuous than the average MMPI-2 test taker. Specifically, his score is just above the high typical threshold score of 65. Concomitantly, his K and S scales are at or near the top of the typical response range for MMPI-2 test takers. This combination of responses, when viewed in unison, may suggest someone who is highly virtuous with many strong religious morals and traditional values. Does this match Alex's clinical presentation and the information we gathered from his clinical interview? It does not!

Thus, based on Alex's endorsements that appear to suggest that he has fewer psychological concerns than most and he has extremely high personal ethics, the authors would believe Alex is attempting to present himself in a most favorable light. In other words, when Alex goes to court, he likely wants the counselor to interpret the MMPI-2 results as suggesting Alex as an unjustly accused, nonviolent, honest, hard-working, decent, law-abiding citizen who would never steal heavy-duty road equipment from his former place of employment or harm his wife.

In fact, Alex would like his MMPI-2 endorsements to suggest that he is the kind of outstanding citizen who was probably painting, repairing, and improving the heavy-duty equipment housed on his property before he returned it to his former employer and kindly supporting his wife without threats or violence.

Now let's review Alex's MMPI-2 Clinical Scales. Typically, the authors find when a client like Alex endorses high correction scores on K and S, the actual psychopathology levels will be higher than indicated on the MMPI-2 Clinical Scales. Stated differently, higher K and S scores reduce the reported pathology levels on the clinical scales. Thus, moderately depressed or anxious clients will appear as only slightly depressed or anxious on their profiles.

Alex's One Scale: Hypochon-driasis is unremarkable. According to this profile, his endorsed items place him in the low average range. Interestingly, Alex's Two Scale: Depression, although falling within the higher end of the normal range, suggests that Alex might be experiencing a twinge of sadness or anxiety. This is less likely a result of remorse or compunction for unlawful behaviors and more likely a twinge of sadness that he was caught and will go to jail or pay a steep fine.

This Two Scale may increase if he is convicted for crimes. Again, the identified "sadness" will likely not be related to compunction for stealing. Instead, these scores would likely reflect his "sadness" that he has to do jail time. Stated differently, Alex, if convicted and required to enter prison and pay a hefty fine, will feel more depressed that he will have lost his freedom and has to pay his "hard-earned" money than feel sad that he had violated the rights of others.

Alex's Three Scale: Hysteria, is relatively unremarkable and fails within the high side of the normal range. Based on the authors' experiences with persons qualifying for antisocial personality disorder, this tad higher score well within the normal range may be related to Alex's rather flamboyant, socially skilled, and talkative mannerism.

However, Alex's Four Scale: Psychopathic Deviate is quite remarkable. This is his highest clinical score along with his Nine Scale: Mania. This elevated Four Scale by itself suggests Alex has endorsed items in a fashion similar to persons fulfilling criteria for antisocial personality disorder.

Specifically, this suggests Alex likely tends to take advantage of others, engage in unlawful behaviors, and be self-centered. Further, the elevated Four Scale indicates that Alex is likely adventure seeking, impulsive, and has difficulties with authority figures.

However, when one looks at both Alex's elevated Four Scale and his elevated Nine Scale: Mania it would suggest that Alex is rebellious, disinhibited, socially skilled and charming. He understands how to gain peoples' trust and then exploit that trust or use information divulged by those who trusted the "charming guy" to later intimidate others.

In addition, he has a sense of personal entitlement. Thus, he likely feels he is "better" or "superior" to others and uses his gift of charm and wit to support his feelings of entitlement. The 4-9 two-point code also suggests he is impulsive, manipulative, and can become hostile when he perceives either real or imagined threats.

Of course, one should never diagnosis someone as fulfilling antisocial personality disorder merely on an elevated Four Scale on the MMPI-2 or any instrument. However, when we consider Alex's MMPI-2 scores in light of his previous clinical interview with the counselor and Alex's reported history, the antisocial personality disorder certainly appears to be a viable diagnosis.

Some might simply overlook Alex's lower than normal Five Scale: Masculinity-Femininity. However, the authors believe comment is warranted. This lower than normal score suggests that Alex likely presents as robustly masculine. He clearly is acculturated into presenting like a "man's man" and likely uses this persona to both gain acceptance and later to intimidate others.

Regarding Alex's Scale Six: Paranoia, his two highest Clinical Scale scores are 4 and 9. As previously mentioned, Alex qualifies for a 4-9 two-point code and has been diagnosed with antisocial personality disorder. Interestingly, there exists a 4-6 two-point code.

However, Alex does not qualify for the 4-6 code, because of his robustly higher and clinically significant 4-9 scores. Although the authors' are unaware of a 4-9-6 three-point code, discussion of Alex's 4-9-6 scoring is warranted. The authors' believe Alex's elevated Scale Six likely is at least partly influenced by his pending court arraignment and possible upcoming court sanctions. Honestly, who wouldn't be at least slightly vigilant or anxious not knowing what others will be doing "to you" based on one's upcoming court case?

4-6 two-point coded persons typically blame others for their problems and brood about their situation. Our strong suspicion is that Alex is in fact doing the same thing, and although he typically can contain his anger, as the stress builds he likely may struggle with his anger containment and may act out especially towards those he blames for prosecuting him. Thus, Catherine, Alex's wife who filed domestic violence charges may be at increased risk for retaliation.

Next is Alex's Seven Scale: Psychasthenia. Folks who typically present as anxious and worried often have higher scores on this scale. Alex's score is in the low normal range. Given his personality, instead of acting or being anxious, his previous scores suggest he is a "man's man," has the ability to influence others via his significant charm and social skills, and to intimidate others whenever necessary. Thus, his lower-normal range score makes sense. Why be anxious when he can control others via his conning and intimidating behaviors?

In addition, regarding the Seven Scale, higher scores may suggest persons who are anxious regarding their milieu. Thus, they often attempt to reduce their anxiety by being highly organized, meticulous, and perfectionist. Alex, on the other hand, is likely impulsive and spontaneous. He may not fully think things out before acting. Hence, his lower-normal range seems logical and supportive of his other MMPI-2 scores and clinical presentation.

Although Alex's Eight Scale: Schizophrenia score is in the middle of the normal range and unremarkable, his Nine Scale: Mania is far above the normal range and clinically significant. Given that Alex denies hallucinations and during his clinical interview he was oriented times three (i.e., person, place, time), engaging, and socially confident, his higher score does not indicate that he is in a manic phase of bipolar disorder or schizophrenic.

Instead, the authors' believe Alex's scores simply reflect his egocentric energy, flamboyant and outgoing personality, and social confidence. This seems supported by Alex's 10 Scale: Social Introversion as well. High scores on this scale would suggest persons who are uncomfortable around others. This clearly is not the case with Alex. He thrives on "the con" and being the center of attention for personal gain.

After reviewing the client's Validity Scores and individual Clinical Scores, we would typically look for two- or three-point codes. In this case, the authors have already discussed Alex's 4-9 two-point code with his antisocial personality disorder diagnosis. However, if the Supplemental or Other Scores via the Extended MMPI-s Report had been purchased, a review of these scores would be helpful.

In Alex's case, because of the counselor's clinical diagnosis of alcohol use disorder for Alex and the high probability that the counselor may be asked to either author a letter regarding his clinical findings to the court or testify in court, he may be particularly interested in the Supplemental Addictions Scale such as the MAC-R, APS, and AAS as well as the additional PSY-5 Scale. Specifically, the results of Alex's endorsements on these scales could be used to supplement the counselor's diagnosis of Alex to the court.

Thus, if the MAC-R, APS, and AAS supported the counselor's alcohol use disorder diagnosis, Alex's legal counsel couldn't merely call the counselor's clinical judgment into question. The counselor would say that his findings were supported by Alex's MAC-R, APS, and AAS scores, as well as the MMPI-2's overall findings.

Conversely, should the counselor's clinical diagnosis not align with the MAC-R, APS, and AAS, the counselor should reevaluate the assigned diagnosis to make certain the diagnosis remains the most accurate for Alex.

If after reevaluation of the clinical assessment interview and the MAC-R, APS, AAS, and MMPI-2 findings, the counselor believes a diagnosis change is warranted, he should do so.

However, if after reevaluation the counselor believes the initial clinical diagnosis was in fact the most accurate, he should be able to explain why the diagnosis assigned is the most accurate diagnosis and how Alex's endorsements may have reflected either something different or influenced the scoring in a particular manner.

Think for a moment. Had you been Alex's counselor and assigned an alcohol use disorder diagnosis after a very thorough clinical assessment interview with Alex and one or more of his significant others, and yet Alex's MMPI-2 scores, including his MAC-R, APS, and AAS scores, had suggested something different, where might you first begin to look on the MMPI-2 to explain why Alex's MMPI-2 did not assess him as fulfilling your assigned diagnosis? Exactly! You would begin by reviewing his Validity Scale Scores.

Specifically, if Alex's combination of F scores were very low and his K and L scores were very high, it would suggest that Alex's profile might be invalid and that he may have been attempting to present himself in a very positive and virtuous manner. If this was not the case, are you certain it was Alex who completed the MMPI-2?

On occasion, the first author has known of counselors who gave clients assessment instruments to complete at home or in the waiting room lobby. Sometimes the returned instruments were highly suspect.

You should always have the client complete the MMPI-2 in the counselor's office without others' potential input into question stems.

Remember, any assessment instrument should be viewed as augmenting the counselor's diagnosis. Stated differently, the counselor's clinical judgment always trumps the assessment instrument's outcome. The counseling professional is the one who diagnoses the client. Assessment instruments do not diagnose clients. Instead, they merely support the counselor's diagnosis of the client or provide additional information that may warrant further investigation and reevaluation of the final diagnosis.

Should the counselor's diagnoses seem to frequently be at odds with assessment instrument outcomes, clinical supervision may be helpful. Here, the clinical supervisor can help the counselor better understand the incongruence and help ensure that the most accurate diagnosis is used.

General MMPI-2-RF Overview

Ben-Porath and Tellegen (2008) developed the MMPI-2-RF. This instrument is a revised version of the MMPI-2. Thus, there exist similarities between the two instruments. The intent of this description is to highlight some of these differences and to help the reader become familiar with this superior instrument.

This said, one of the most evident differences between the MMPI-2 and the MMPI-2-RF is instrument length. Specifically, the MMPI-2-RF is significantly shorter. The MMPI-2-RF is composed of only 338 true–false items. These same questions were used in the MMPI-2.

However, the MMPI-2-RF restructured the questions and eliminated over 200 MMPI-2 questions. The result is an instrument with scoring based on 50 scales. Ben-Porath and Tellegen, 2008 (p. 1) reported the instrument was designed to be a "broad-band instrument intended for use in a variety of settings" (Ben-Porath & Tellegen, 2008, p. 1).

The MMPI-2-RF was developed for persons 18 years of age and older, and was first published in 2008 (Pearson, 2011b). The MMPI-2-RF requires a fifth-grade or higher reading level. The anticipated completion time for MMPI-2-RF is 35 to 50 minutes, and it can be administered via paper-and-pencil test, CD, or computer administration (Pearson, 2011b). Pearson states, "The MMPI-2-RF provides a valuable alternative to the MMPI-2 test, not a replacement....
The MMPI-2-RF aids clinicians in the assessment of mental disorders, identification of specific problem areas, and treatment planning in a variety of settings" (Pearson, 2011b). Pearson indicates purchasers must qualify at the "C-Level" (Pearson, 2011b). The MMPI-2RF can be ordered directly from Pearson at 1-800-627-7271.

MMPI-2-RF Reliability and Validity. One-week test–retest coefficients for the MMPI-2-RF validity scales based on the MMPI-2 normative sample ranged between .40 and .84 for men and women with an internal consistency (alpha) for men between .37 and .69 and for women .20 to .71 (Tellegen & Ben-Porath, 2008, p. 23). Regarding Clinical Scales, Tellegen and Ben-Porath (2008, p. 32) state,

> With the exception of the original Clinical Scales, no other MMPI or MMPI-2 scales have been as extensively validated against a variety of criteria in as broad a range of settings as have the MMPI-2-RF scales.

The MMPI-2-RF Technical Manual (Tellegen & Ben-Porath, 2008) is filled with a plethora of assorted tables supporting their claim.

MMPI-2-RF Scales. The MMPI-2-RF has nine Validity Scales and 42 Substantive Scales. MMPI-2-RF Validity Scales include the following: (a) Variable Response Inconsistency (random responding), (b) True Response Inconsistency (fixed responding), (c) Infrequent Responses (responses that are atypical from the main sample of responses), (d) Infrequent Psychopathology Responses (responses that are atypical in psychiatric populations), (e) Infrequent Somatic Responses (responses atypical in medical populations), (f) Symptom Validity (bodily and cognitive complaints often associated with over reporting), (g) Response Bias Scale, (h) Uncommon Virtues (infrequently reported moral thinking or behaving), and (i) Adjustment Validity (proclamation of good psychological functioning associated with under reporting) scales (Pearson, 2011b; Tellegen & Ben-Porath, 2008, p. 6).

Tellegen and Ben-Porath (2008, p. 16) also created three Higher-Order Scales that are included in the MMPI-2-RF. These are broad areas and include Emotional/Internalizing Dysfunction (problems specific to mood and affect), Thought Dysfunction (disordered thinking), and Behavioral/Externalizing Dysfunction (problems resulting from under controlled behaviors; (Tellegen & Ben-Porath, 2008, p. 6). The intent behind these Higher-Order Scales was to establish a set of narrowly focused measures that are clinically meaningful and serve an integrative function (Tellegen & Ben-Porath, 2008, p. 16).

Unlike the MMPI-2, the MMPI-2-RF does not use the 10 Clinical Scales. Instead, the MMPI-2-RF only uses the Restructured Clinical Scales. As you will remember from the earlier MMPI-2 description, the Restructured Clinical Scales include (a) Demoralization (general life dissatisfaction and unhappiness), (b) Somatic Complaints (vague bodily complaints), (c) Low Positive Emotions (a lack of positive emotional responsiveness), (d) Cynicism (overall distrust and low opinion of others), (e) Antisocial Behavior (rule breaking and irresponsible behaviors), (f) Ideas of Persecution (perceptions that others are out to harm the client), (g) Dysfunctional Negative Emotions (anxiety, anger, irritability), (h) Aberrant Experiences (atypical thinking or perceptions), and (i) Hypomanic Activation (over activation, aggression, impulsivity, and grandiosity; Ben-Porath & Tellegen, 2008, p. 6).

Internalizing Scales in the MMPI-2-RF are specific to the client's internalized experiences and perceptions. These include the following: (a) Suicidal/Death Ideation (direct reports of suicidal ideation and recent attempts), (b) Helplessness/Hopelessness (perceptions that goals are unattainable and problems will never be resolved), (c) Self-Doubt (a lack of confidence and feelings of uselessness), (d) Inefficacy (perceptions of self-inefficacious-ness and indecisiveness), (e) Stress/Worry (rumination and focus on disappointments and time pressure stressors), (f) Anxiety (pervasive anxiety, frights, and frequent night terrors), (g) Anger Proness (becoming easily angered and impatient), (h) Behavior-Restricting Fears (fears that stop or truncate daily activities), and (i) Multiple Specific Fears (fears of blood, fire, thunder, and so forth; Ben-Porath & Tellegen, 2008, p. 6).

Conversely, Externalizing MMPI-2-RF Scales are experiences within the external environment. These Externalizing Scales include (a) Juvenile Conduct Problems (difficulties at school and home or stealing), (b) Substance Abuse (current and past alcohol and drug abuse), (c) Aggression (physically aggressive and violent behaviors), and (d) Activation (heightened excitation and energy level; Ben-Porath & Tellegen, 2008, p. 7).

Interpersonal Scales on the MMPI-2-RF include: (a) Family Problems (conflictual family relationships), (b) Interpersonal Passivity (unassertiveness and submissiveness), (c) Social Avoidance (not enjoying and avoiding social experiences), (d) Shyness-Bashful (feeling inhibited and anxious in social contexts), and (e) Disaffiliativeness (disliking people and disliking being around others; Ben-Porath & Tellegen, 2008, p. 7). In addition, the MMPI-2-RF uses the PSY-5. Ben-Porath and Tellegen (2008, p. 58) state, "The MMPI-2-RF PSY-5 Scales are updated versions of the five MMPI-2 scales...all five scales both low and high scores are interpretable as such." Thus, the MMPI-2-RF uses updated PSY-5 Scales in comparison to the MMPI-2 and the term "low" reflects either an absence or limited presence of the corresponding scales psychological construct and "high" reflects significant presence of the corresponding scales psychological construct.

Kenesha's MMPI-2-RF Profile

The review of the MMPI-2-RF will be somewhat similar to the MMPI-2 described with Alex. We will start with the Validity Scales. The Validity Scales set the stage. If they suggest the test taker endorsed a suspect or invalid test, the other scales provide little if any relevant information. Once it is determined that the test taker endorsed the MMPI-2-RF in a fashion similar to others who were invested in the assessment process, we can review important other scales.

When the authors review MMPI-2-RF scores, they review Higher-Order Scales first. This provides a broad interpretation of the client's overall functioning and the types of chief presenting issues.

Next, the authors review the Restructured Clinical Scales and PSY-5. These scales provide a more in-depth description of the client's chief presenting concerns and personality characteristics. This is followed by a review of the Internalizing, Externalizing, and Interpersonal scales. Finally, they review the Specific Problem Scales and if warranted Interest Scales.

Now let's look at Kenesha's Validity Scale Scores contained within Table 3.2.

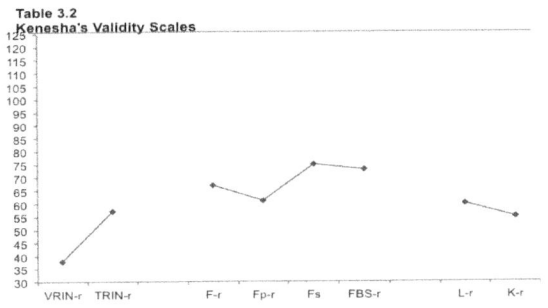

Table 3.2
Kenesha's Validity Scales

We first start with Kenesha's VRIN-r Scale score, 38. High scores on the VRIN-r make the test uninterruptable, because the test taker had excessive response inconsistency. In Kenesha's case, we visually see that her 38 score is below the 50-point line and is low. This suggests that Kenesha endorsed question responses in a consistent manner and the test is interpretable. Next, we review Kenesha's TRIN-r score, 57.

Again, Kenesha endorsed responses in a manner that suggests the test is interpretable. Had she scored excessively high or low on this scale, her endorsements would have suggested that she intentionally attempted to misrepresent herself and the test would not be interpretable. Kenesha scored 67 on the F-r. This is a low score. It suggests that Kenesha did not over report her complaints.

Extremely high scores over 120 would suggest that even if presenting with severe psychological difficulties, the test taker is over reporting an excessive number of infrequent responses (Ben-Porath & Tellegen, 2008, p. 26). The same is true with Kenesha's Fp-r, Fs, and FBS-r Scale scores. Her respective low scores of 61, 75, and 73 all suggest that Kenesha did not over report her symptoms or psychopathology.

The opposite problem of over reporting psychological symptoms is underreporting. Here, the client attempts to minimize psychological problems or present him- or herself in a most favorable light.

Kenesha's scores on scales designed to identify underreporting, L-r and K-r, are low (i.e., 60 and 55). Thus, based on Kenesha's Validity Scale scores it appears that Kenesha was invested in the test-taking process, consistent in her responses, and approached the test in an honest and forthright manner. In nonprofessional terms, she did not attempt to "Fake Good" or "Fake Bad." The result is an interpretable and valid appearing test.

Higher-Order Scales

Higher-Order Scales demonstrate "clinically important individual variations in the basic domains of affect, thought, and action" (Ben-Porath & Tellegen, 2008, p. 32). Stated differently, these Higher-Order Scales provide an overview of the client's general functioning according to affect, thought, and action.

Although individual RC Scales may identify greater levels of psychopathology or functioning, the Higher-Order Scales provide a general idea of what major area(s) the client is experiencing psychological distress or difficulties.

The first scale that we review is the Emotional/Internalizing Dysfunction (EID) Scale. Here, Kenesha scores a moderately high score of 77.

Table 3.3
Kenesha's Higher-Order and Restructured Clinical Scales

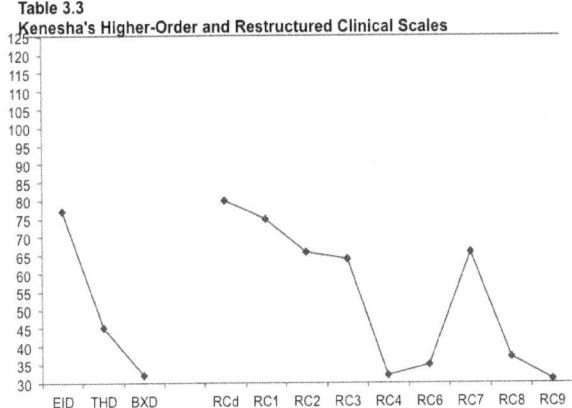

Her score suggests she clearly is experiencing significant emotional distress. A score of 80 would indicate that the degree of distress experienced would likely be perceived by the client as a crisis. Thus, her score is very close to "crisis levels." Her score suggestions she likely feels overwhelmed, pessimistic about the future, helpless to change the emotional feelings she is experiencing, and depressed.

Given the length of time, Kenesha has been remaining in her unsatisfactory relationship with her spouse, living with her spouse in a small apartment, and the length of time she has experienced her reported anxiety, her moderately high, but not crisis, score seems logical. Stated differently, she likely has become familiar and accustomed with the psychological distress because of the length of time she has had these experiences.

The next two Higher-Order Scales to review include the Thought Dysfunction Scale and the Behavioral/Externalizing Dysfunction Scale. Kenesha scores low on both (45 and 32). Her low score on the Thought Dysfunction Scale suggests she is thinking logically and coherently. In other words, she does not present with psychotic features.

Furthermore, her Behavioral/Externalizing Dysfunction Scale Score (32) suggests she is unlikely to be violent, abuse alcohol or other drugs, or have poor impulse control. Stated differently, Kenesha demonstrates significant impulse control and is likely an outstanding citizen who strictly follows expected social norms and rules.

Just as an aside, and given your knowledge of Alex, would you anticipate Alex would score "high" or "low" on the Behavioral/Externalizing Dysfunction Scale? Great response! You are

100% correct! He would score "high." Alex's high score would suggest that he had poor impulse control.

Restructured Clinical Scales

Next, the authors move to the Restructured Clinical Scales (Table 3.3) and start with the Demoralization Scale (RCd). The Demoralization Scale indicates the client's general life unhappiness and dissatisfaction.

Given your knowledge of Kenesha from the clinical interview and her diagnosis, would you anticipate her score would be low or high on this scale? In other words, would you believe Kenesha has general happiness and life satisfaction (low score) or do you believe she has general unhappiness and life dissatisfaction (high score)? Kenesha actually scores at the lowest end of the "high" score with an 80. This suggests she is experiencing robust emotional turmoil in her life, she is feeling overwhelmed, and she is extremely dissatisfied.

As we review the remainder of the Restructured Clinical Scales, we will use Kenesha's Demoralization Scale as a backdrop to help keep the individual scale scores in perspective.

As an aside and given Kenesha's score is high, the counselors will also need to review her Suicide Scale and minimally query Kenesha about possible suicidal ideation or intent. The counselor would also provide a 24-hour helpline number she can call should she feel overwhelmed, ask how she would kill herself if she intended to, and remove or eliminate the suicide instrument (e.g., gun) from her immediate environment.

Then, the counselor would document within her case notes Kenesha's responses, the counselor's responding interventions, and Kenesha's agreement to the same, or involuntary hospitalization or other necessary least restrictive environment (Juhnke, Granello, & Granello, 2010; Juhnke, Juhnke, & Hsieh, 2012).

At this point in the MMPI-2-RF review process, we will complete the review of each of the remaining Restructured Clinical Scales. Because this was also demonstrated in the MMPI-2 review, the authors will provide only a succinct review here.

If you review Table 3.3 and Kenesha's individual Restructured Scale Scores, you will find that Kenesha presents with a score of 75 on the Somatic Complaints Scale (RC1). This is a moderately high score and suggests that Kenesha may well complain of headaches, gastrointestinal problems, or other physical complaints related to her anxiety and distress.

Her Low Positive Emotions Scale (RC2) has a high score (66). This reflects her overall pessimism that things will improve, that she likely is socially introverted and socially disengaged from others. It further suggests that she lacks energy and may qualify for a disorder such as major depression.

Kenesha's Cynicism Scale (RC3) score is 64. This score is a moderate score and just one point from a high score. Persons with similar scores may feel alienated from others and possibly distrustful of others.

Kenesha's Antisocial Behavior Scale (RC4) should not surprise us. Her 32 score is far below average and suggests that she likely has not participated in criminal activity, that she does not endorse items similar to those who are diagnosed with antisocial personality disorder, and that her endorsements do not appear to reflect past or present substance-using behaviors.

Kenesha does not appear to have persecutory, paranoid delusions, or psychotic features as evidenced by her respective low scores of 35 and 37 on her Ideas of Persecution Scale (RC6) and Aberrant Experiences Scale (RC8).

However, her dysfunctional Negative Emotions Scale (RC7) score of 66 is high and suggests she may excessively worry, be guilt prone, and self-critical; her low Hypomanic Activation Scale (RC9) score (31) suggests she has below expected activation and engagement within her environment.

PSY-5. Table 3.4 provides Kenesha's PSY-5 scores and a graphic representation of her scores. Here, Kenesha's Aggressiveness—Revised (AGGR-r) Scale score is 35. This score suggests Kenesha is passive and submissive in her relationships with others, whereas scores above 65 are reflective of persons who are overly assertive, socially dominant, and viewed by others as domineering—clearly not a match for Kenesha's personality.

Her Psychoticism—Revised (PSYC-r) scale score is 32 and also quite low. Such a low score suggests an absence of thought disturbances.

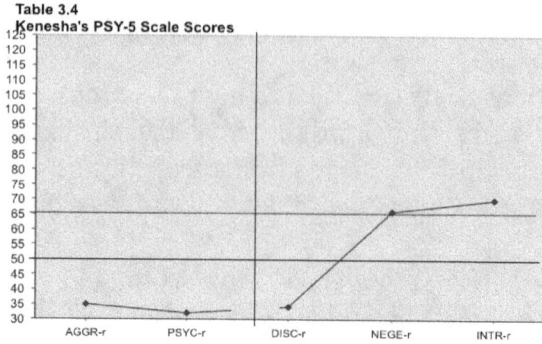

Table 3.4
Kenesha's PSY-5 Scale Scores

Kenesha's score of 34 on the Disconstraint—Revised (DISC-r) Scale suggests she is overly constrained in her behaviors. High scores of 65 and above on this scale would suggest that one acts impulsively, and is sensation seeking.

The next PSY-5 scale is the Negative Emotionality/ Neuroticism—Revised (NEGE-r) Scale. Kenesha's score of 66 is high on this scale and suggests she experiences significant anxiety, insecurity, and worry. As well, Kenesha's score of 70 on the Introversion/Low Positive Emotionality—Revised (INTR-r) Scale suggests Kenesha likely avoids social situations and is socially introverted.

Internalizing, Externalizing, and Interpersonal Scales. Although some may argue that the review of these scales should be reviewed before the PSY-5, the authors find it helpful to review these Internalizing, Externalizing, and Interpersonal scales (Tables 3.5 and 6) after the PSY-5. This review starts with the Internalizing Scale Suicidal/Death Ideation (SUI).

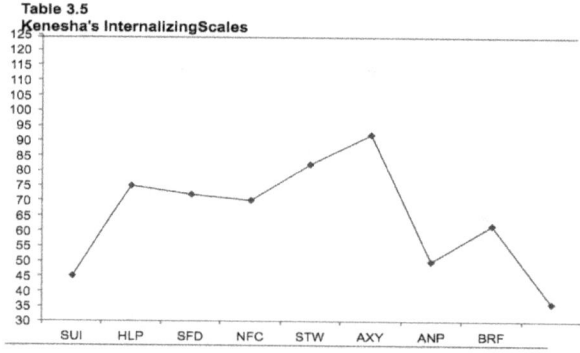

Table 3.5
Kenesha's Internalizing Scales

As previously mentioned, this is an important scale to investigate given Kenesha's elevated Demoralization Scale score. Interestingly,

Kenesha scores low (45) on the Suicidal/Death Ideation Scale. Thus, she endorses few if any items suggesting either suicide or death intent. Going back to Kenesha's clinical interview, she stated significant religiosity and her mother's strong "Baptist" presence.

Although it is not impossible for those with significant religiosity or from Baptist backgrounds (or any other religious backgrounds) to commit suicide, Kenesha seems to take pride and comfort in her religious upbringing. Because suicide is broadly believed to be a sin of commission within most religions, Kenesha may perceive that suicide is an unacceptable behavior that would result in eternal banishment to Hell.

This may well reflect why her Suicidal/Death Ideation Scale is low. Whatever the reason for her low Suicidal/Death Ideation Scale score, the counselor should follow the suicide assessment and intervention protocol described earlier, to ensure that Kenesha is safe and knows how to contact help, should she begin to experience suicidal ideation.

Kenesha's endorsements on the Helplessness/Hopelessness (HLP) Scale are in the moderate middle (75; Table 3.5). Persons endorsing similar items feel hopeless and pessimistic regarding their future, and often believe they cannot be helped. This appears to be a solid match to Kenesha's clinical presentation.

Kenesha's Self-Doubt (SFD) scale score of 72 suggests she experiences self-doubt, lacks self-confidence, and feels useless. It further suggests that she is prone to rumination and intropunitive thinking (Ben-Perth & Tellegen, 2008, p. 48). Kenesha's Inefficacy (NFC) Scale score of 70 and her Stress/Worry (STW) Scale score of 82 suggest she is predominantly passive, indecisive, inefficacious, prone to worry, and overly reactive to perceived stressful situations; she may ruminate on worrisome or stressful events (Ben-Perth & Tellegen, 2008, p. 48).

As one would expect, Kenesha's Anxiety (AXY) Scale is in the moderately high area (92) and is eight points from a high score (Table 3.5). This scale is congruent and supports other MMPI-2-RF scales specific to anxiety and anxious behaviors. The Anxiety Scale suggests that Kenesha reports anxious feelings and endorses anxiety-related concerns. Her anxiety is significant enough to cause difficulties sleeping, and she likely benefits from her antianxiety medications.

Regarding her last three Internalizing Scales—Anger Proneness (ANP), Behavior-Restricting Fears (BRF), and Multiple Specific Fears

(MSF)—Kenesha's scores are unremarkable (Table 3.5). Her scores fall below noted psychopathology distress levels at 50, 62, and 36, respectively. Thus, Kenesha's scores suggest she rarely becomes impatient or annoyed by others and does not appear to fulfill the diagnostic requirements for agoraphobia or a specific phobia.

Externalizing Scale scores on Kenesha's Juvenile Conduct Problems (JCP), Substance Abuse (SUB), and Aggression (AGG) scales are all clinically unremarkable and are respectively 50, 40, and 34 (Table 3.6). However, Kenesha's Activation (ACT) Scale score of 37 indicates that the client has below-average levels of energy and potentially may feel tired or exhausted. This seems logical of someone who has been anxious for a long period of time and who has endorsed items suggesting physical aches and pains as Kenesha has on previous MMPI-2-RF scales.

Table 3.6

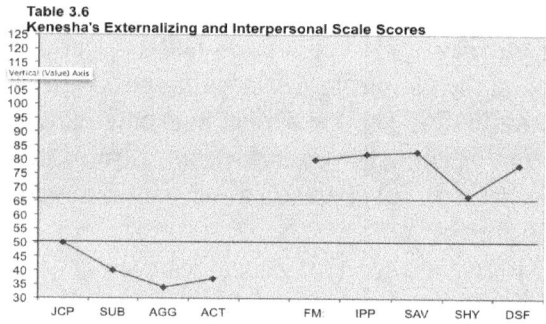

Kenesha's Externalizing and Interpersonal Scale Scores

Kenesha's Interpersonal Scales paint a picture of someone who has robust family relationship stressors and who prefers to be alone rather than in social situations. Her Family Problems (FM:) Scale score is 80 (Table 3.6). This score further suggests that Kenesha feels unsupported and unappreciated by family members, and she believes family members cannot be fully trusted.

The Family Problems Scale further suggests family conflict and blaming of family members for Kenesha's difficulties. Kenesha's Interpersonal Passivity (IPP) Scale score of 82 suggests she is unassertive, fails to stand up for herself, and is unlikely to take charge of situations.

This score is supported by Kenesha's Social Avoidance (SAV) Scale, her Shyness (SHY) Scale, and her Disaffiliativeness (DSF) Scale sores that are 83, 67, and 78, respectively (Table 3.6). These combined scale scores suggest that Kenesha is introverted and shy, dislikes social events, is easily embarrassed, and is uncomfortable around others.

DISCUSSION

This chapter reviewed validity and clinical scales of the MMPI-2 and the MMPI-2-RF. Two and three point codes were discussed. Finally, the chapter provided narrative reviews of Alex's and Kenesha's MMPI-2 and MMPI-2-RF scores.

Chapter 3 Questions

1. Please describe the following scales in your own terms:
   a.   ? Scale:

   b.   L Scale:

   c.   K Scale:

   d.   F Scale:

   e.   One Scale: Hypochondriasis

   f.   Two Scale: Depression

   g.   Three Scale: Hysteria

   h.   Four Scale: Psychopathic Deviate

   i.   Five Scale: Masculinity – Femininity

   j.   Six Scale: Paranoia

   k.   Seven Scale: Psychasthenia

   l.   Eight Scale: Schizophrenia

   m.   Nine Scale: Mania

   n.   Ten (0) Scale: Social Introversion

2. Describe what two and three-point codes are and one or two that are likely prevalent with the clinical population you serve or wish to serve.

3. What is Alex's two-point code and what may it suggest about him?

Chapter 4:
Reporting Results

Over the years we have found it useful to begin with validity scales. This is especially true with nondefensive, unguarded clients, such as Ms. Kenesha Battle Williams. A few statements reporting her honest and truthful responses, is a good way to reduce client anxiety and promote thoughtful consideration of later clinical implications.

Counselor:

Kenesha, it is clear you invested yourself in this test taking experience, answered all 567 test questions and responded in a truthful and honest manner. You did not attempt to misrepresent yourself. Congratulations to you, Kenesha, for your diligence and truthfulness.

Conversely, if the test taker failed to answer sufficient questions or haphazardly or incongruently responded to test questions, this is the best time to indicate the responses were insufficient or incongruent and therefore the results were uninterpretable. If the missed questions have a common theme (i.e., suicide, hallucinations, etc.), it would be important to verbally review the questions with the client and determine if additional assessment or intervention specific to the topic is warranted.

Again, if the testee was unguarded and nondefensive, like Kenesha, we would ask what the testee believes the test indicated. We then would "triangulate" the three sources of information—information from the clinical interview, information from what the testee "believes" the test revealed, and information resulting from the MMPI-2 or MMPI-2-RF.

In Kenesha's case, we anticipate she would state the test results indicate she is anxious. This would match Kenesha's clinical interview and her MMPI-2-RF test results. We would then review the client's most elevated clinical scores. For example, given Kenesha's elevated EID score we would discuss her endorsements of significant emotional distress and the likelihood that she is feeling overwhelmed, pessimistic about the future, and depressed. Thus, the counselor might say...

Counselor:

Your MMPI endorsements suggest the anxiety you're experiencing is pretty over-whelming at times. It further suggests you likely feel depressed, and view the future with pessimism and angst. Is that a match for you, Kenesha?

If Kenesha reports the test results and her perceptions match, we would ask Kenesha if she believed addressing her anxiety would be a relevant goal for her treatment. If she agreed, we would seek her input to help create her desired outcomes. Should Kenesha disagree with incorporating a goal specific to anxiety in her treatment plan we might say something like...

Counselor:

I guess I'm a little confused, Kenesha. During our clinical interview you reported anxiety as your major concern. And, the items you endorsed on the MMPI suggest you are experiencing anxiety. How is it helpful not to include a treatment goals specific to anxiety?

Such questioning can help clients gain insight into the need to address their pressing concerns. We would continue reviewing Kenesha's most elevated scale scores until an agreeable treatment plan was created that addressed the majority of her concerns.

Things are different in the case of Mr. Alex Smith. Alex is defensive and guarded. During Alex's clinical interview Alex denied any treatment goals and indicated his attorney encouraged him to initiate the counseling process to receive a "reduced sentence". Stated differently, unlike Kenesha who openly described her pressing concerns in a non-defensive and unguarded manner, Alex denied problems or concerns.

Second, he naively reported anticipated secondary gains for entering treatment. Kenesha reported no such secondary gains and perceived benefits to change.

Third, unlike Kenesha, Alex's validity scales have inflated L and K scores. As indicated in the previous chapter, such scale elevations suggest someone is either highly virtuous with strong religious morals and traditional values or someone is attempting to present self in a most positive and favorable manner.

Given Alex's clinical presentation, Dr. Juhnke's diagnosis of Antisocial Personality Disorder for Alex, and Alex's 4-9 two-point code, we would not begin with Alex's validity scores nor would we ask Alex about his perceptions of the test outcome. Instead, we would begin by reporting Alex's two-point codes and any additionally elevated clinical scales. This would first be done in a nonpathological and "safe" manner and then progress to more difficult topics. Here, we would begin by reframing Alex's 4-9 two-point code something like this…

Counselor:

Alex, your test endorsements suggest you often are energetic and frequently seek excitement and adventure. Do you think that's a fairly accurate description of you?

If Alex agreed, we would likely increase the threshold by asking something like…

Counselor:

Have you ever found your seeking excitement or adventure problematic?

If Alex indicated "yes", we would have him explain what happened and what he learned from those behaviors. We might further ask…

Counselor:

Your MMPI endorsements further suggest that at times others may have perceived you as a "rule breaker" or as someone who has difficulties complying with people in authority. Can you tell me a little more about that?

Again, we would move through the elevated two- and three-point codes first, and then ask about elevated clinical scores one through 10. The focus is to both provide an opportunity for the client to discuss presenting concerns and to generate treatment goals the client wishes to accomplish via counseling.

Chapter 4 Questions

1. Describe when and why you might respond to the testee's validity codes first?

2. Describe when you would not address the testee's validity codes first? Why?

3. How do you decide when to address two- or three-point codes?

4. What clinical scores do you address and how do you determine in what order to ask about elevated clinical scores?

5. What might you wish to do if the test taker failed to answer questions specific to a topic like suicide?

Chapter 5:
Concluding Remarks

We trust you have found this book on the MMPI-2 and MMPI-2-RF helpful to your clients and you. The intent of this book was to increase your knowledge of both instruments so you could better help your clients. Always ensure you utilize only assessment instruments that you have been adequately trained and supervised.

Remember, one can only utilize assessment instruments that match the scope of practice your state license allows and complies with your professional association's assessment ethics.

As well, assessment instrument scores alone should not be used to diagnose clients. We strongly believe diagnosis minimally requires a clinical interview. Assessment instrument results merely augment one's clinical judgement and can be used to support one's diagnosis of a client.

Remember too that assessment instrument scores only suggest that a testee has responded in a manner similar to persons with suggested diagnoses. In other words, it does not mean that the testee actually fulfills the diagnosis criteria.

Chapter 5 Questions

1. What do "scope of practice" laws for the state in which you are licensed indicate regarding your use of "Class C" Personality Assessments instruments?

2. What do your professional association ethics codes say regarding your use of "Class C" Personality Assessment instruments?

3. According to Juhnke and Balkin, what must happen to diagnose a client? Explain why you agree or disagree.

4. Do testees who score similarly to persons diagnosed with certain DSM-5 diagnoses on the MMPI-2 or MMPI-2-RF mean the testee has the same diagnosis? Explain.

References

American Psychiatric Association. (2013). Diagnostic and statistical manual of mental disorders (5th ed.). Washington, DC: Author.

Ben-Porath, Y. S., & Tellegen, A. (2008). MMPI-2-RF: Manual for administration, scoring, and interpretation. Minneapolis, MN: University of Minnesota Press.

Bubenzer, D. L., Zimpfer, D. G., & Mahrle, C. L. (1990). Standardized individual appraisal in agency and private practice. Journal of Mental Health Counseling, 12, 51–66.

Butcher, J. N., Dahlstrom, W. G., Graham, J. R., Tellegen, A., & Kaemmer, B. (2001). MMPI-2:Minnesota Multiphasic Personality Inventory 2 Manual for administration and scoring. Minneapolis, MN: University of Minneapolis Press.

Drayton, M. (2009). The Minnesota Multiphasic Personality Inventory—2 (MMPI-2). Occupational Medicine, 59(2), 135–136.

Dufrense, R., Laux, J., Tahani, D., & Juhnke, G. A. (in-press). Substance use instruments: 13 years later. (Journal of Addictions & Offender Counseling).

Juhnke, G. A. (2002). Substance abuse assessment: A handbook for mental health Professionals. New York, NY: Brunner-Routledge.

Juhnke, G. A., Granello, D. H., & Granello, P. F. (2010). Suicide, self-injury, and violence in the schools: Assessment, prevention, and intervention strategies. Hoboken, NJ: John Wiley & Sons.

Juhnke, G. A., Juhnke, G. B., & Hsieh, P. (2012). SCATTT: A suicide intervention plan mnemonic for use when clients present suicide intent. Retrieved October 16, 2012 from http://www.counseling.org/Resources/Library/VISTAS/vistas12/Article_34.pdf

Juhnke, G. A., Vacc, N. A., Curtis, R. C., Coll, K. M., & Paredes, D.M. (2003). Assessment instruments used by addictions counselors. Journal of Addictions & Offender Counseling, 23, 66–72.

Kessler, R. C., Chiu, W. T., Demler, O., & Walters, E. E. (2005). Prevalence, severity, and comorbidity of twelve month DSMIV disorders in the National Comorbidity Survey Replication (NCSR). Archives of General Psychiatry. 62, 617–627.

Lenzenweger, M. F., Lane, M. C., Loranger, A. W., & Kessler, R. C. (2007). DSM-IV personality disorders in the National Comorbidity Survey Replication. Biological Psychiatry, 62, 553–564.

Millon, T. (1981). Disorders of Personality: DSM-III Axis II. New York, NY: Wiley—Interscience.

Nichols, D. S. (2001). Essentials of MMPI-2 Assessment. New York, NY: Wiley.

O'Connor, B. P. (2008). Other personality disorders. In M. Hersen & J. Rosqvist (Eds.), Handbook of psychological assessment, case Conceptualization and treatment (Vol. 1; pp. 438–462). Hoboken, NJ: Wiley.

Pearson (2011a). MMPI-2. Retrieved from http://psychcorp.pearsonassessments.com/HAIWEB/Cultures/en-us/Productdetail.htm?Pid=MMPI-2

Pearson. (2011b). MMPI-2-RF retrieved from http://www.pearsonassessments.com/HAIWEB/Cultures/en-us/Productdetail.htm?Pid=PAg523&Mode=summary

Sellbom, M., & Ben-Porath, Y. S. (2005). Mapping the MMPI-2 restructured clinical scales onto normal Personality traits: Evidence of construct validity. Journal of Personality Assessment, 85, 179–187.

Sellbom, M., Ben-Porath, Y. S., Lilienfeld, S. O., Patrick, C. J., & Graham, J. R. (2005). Assessing psychopathic personality traits with the MMPI-2. Journal or Personality Assessment, 85, 334–343.

Tellegen, A., & Ben-Porath, Y. S. (2008). MMPI-2 RF: Technical manual. Minneapolis, MN: University of Minnesota Press.

U.S. Department of Health & Human Services. (2010). 2010 Fact Sheet—Mood disorders. Retrieved from http://report.nih.gov/NIHfactsheets/ViewFactSheet. aspx?csid=48&key=M#M

Vacc, N. A. (1982). A conceptual framework for continuous assessment of clients. Measurement and Evaluation in Guidance, 15, 40–48.

Vacha-Haase, T., Tani, C. R., Kogan, L. R., Woodall, R. A., & Thompson, B. (2001). Reliability generalization: Exploring reliability variations on the MMPI/MMPI-2 validity scale scores. Assessment, 8, 391–401.

Watkins, C. E., Jr., Campbell, V. L., & McGregor, P. (1988). Counseling psychologists' uses of and opinions about psychological tests: A contemporary perspective. Counseling Psychologist, 16, 476–486.

Wise, E. A., Streiner, D. L., & Walfish, S. (2010). A review and comparison of the reliabilities of the MMPI-2, MCMI-III, and PAI presented in their respective test manuals. Measurement and Evaluation in Counseling and Development, 42, 246–254.

About the Authors:

Gerald A. Juhnke, Ed.D., LPC, NCC, MAC, ACS attained his doctorate in Counselor Education and Supervision 1991. He is a Professor and the former founding Doctoral Program Director in the Department of Counseling at The University of Texas at San Antonio (UTSA). Jerry has authored 12 published or in-press academic books. Since 1992, Jerry has also authored or co-authored more than 50-refereed articles, 14 assessment instruments, and pre-sented over 150 professional pre-sentations. Jerry is an American Counseling Association Fellow and Past President of seven professional associations. He is an Associate Editor for the Journal of Counseling and Development, former Editor in Chief of The Journal of Addictions and Offender Counseling, and former Co-Chair of the American Counseling Association's Council of Journal Editors. He has received numerous counseling and teaching awards including the American Counseling Association's David K. Brooks' Distinguished Mentor Award, the American Counseling Association's Ralph F. Berdie Research Award, the International Association for Addictions and Offender Counseling Addictions Educator Excellence Award, the Journal of Addictions and Offender Counseling Research Award, the North Carolina Counseling Association's Professional Writing and Research Award, and The University of North Carolina at Greensboro's School of Education's Teaching Excellence Award.

Jerry's clinical and research experiences span 30 years. His clinical experiences include crisis intervention and intensive in-home family therapy with families where one or more clients fulfilled a dual diagnosis that included both sub-stance misuse and a personality disorder. While at Western Michigan University, Jerry's clinical marriage and family therapy skills were greatly enriched via three-and-a-half years of "live clinical" supervision and mentoring by internationally recognized family therapist and Family Systems/Family-of-Origin expert, Dr. Alan Hovestadt. Alan was the founder of Western Michigan University's Marriage and Family

Therapy Program and department chair, and is a former American Association for Marriage and Family Therapy President. As a junior faculty member at The University of North Carolina at Greensboro (UNCG), Jerry's research and scholarly writing skills were groomed and amplified via the tutelage of Dr. Nicholas Vacc. Jerry's passion for "life-threatening behaviors" intertwines suicide, violence, addictions, and trauma within a research agenda that includes assessment and marriage and family counseling. He is a former Professor and Clinic Director at The University of North Carolina at Greensboro, a former Faculty Fellow for the North Carolina Governor's Institute on Alcohol and Substance Abuse, a former Fellow for UNCG's Division on Youth Aggression and Violence, and a former faculty member for The Michigan Supreme Court's Judicial Institute. He has served as grant author, co-author, co-principal investigator and consultant on multiple grant submissions and external awards totaling more than $1.5 million specific to school violence and substance abuse including a $250,000 United States Congressional grant addressing school violence in the District of Columbia's 15 most violent schools.

Prior to working as an academic and counselor, Jerry was Vice President of Just Fine Foods. There, he gained and demonstrated his financial management, budgeting, and organizational skills while serving an incredible team of more than 118 people who dedicated themselves to co-creating dining experiences of excellence for patrons at two family owned and operated restaurants and the events they catered. As Vice President of Just Fine Foods, President of seven professional associations, principal investigator and consultant on multiple grants, Chair of the UTSA's Faculty Grievance Committee, Chair of UNCG's Graduate Studies Council Subcommittee on Graduate Curriculum, and Program Coordinator for both UNCG's Marriage and Family Counseling Educational Specialist Track and Substance Abuse/Addictions Counseling Educational Specialist Track, Jerry became adept at strategically identifying and capitalizing upon team strengths, and executing profitable business, association, and educational ventures these teams could accomplish better than competitors.

Jerry's perceptions of leadership were greatly influenced by Dr. William Watson Purkey, the founder of Invitational Education Theory. From 1992 to 2004 and beyond, Dr. Purkey mentored Jerry, and the duo co-presented throughout the country and co-authored multiple papers on the use of Invitational Leadership.

Rick Balkin, Ph.D., LPCC, NCC is a Professor at the University of Mississippi and the former Doctoral Program Coordinator at the University of Louisville. Dr. Balkin is a Fellow of the American Counseling Association, the editor for the Journal of Counseling and Development, the flagship journal for the American Counseling Association, and past president for the Association for Assessment and Research in Counseling. He serves on numerous committees for ACA.

Dr. Balkin has over 70 publications, which include text books on assessment in counseling and soon to be published textbook on research, published tests and technical manuals, peer-reviewed manuscripts, book chapters, and conference proceedings. His counseling experience with at-risk youth was formative to his research agenda, which includes understanding the role of counseling and relevant goals for adolescents in crisis and counseling outcomes. This led to numerous published articles and one published measure through Mindgarden (Crisis Stabilization Scale) related to assessing and counseling at-risk youth.

He has published in the area of religious diversity and forgiveness and developed a model and measure for counseling clients through issues of forgiveness and conflict.

www.ingramcontent.com/pod-product-compliance
Lightning Source LLC
Chambersburg PA
CBHW062103280526
45788CB00003B/1338